D0493029

THIS IS
WHY I
RESIST

DR SHOLA MOS-SHOGBAMIMU

THIS IS WHY I RESIST

HEADLINE

First published in 2021 by
HEADLINE PUBLISHING GROUP

1

Cataloguing in Publication Data is available from the British Library

Hardback ISBN 978 1 4722 8076 3
Trade paperback ISBN 978 1 4722 8077 0

Typeset in Arno Pro by CC Book Production

Printed and bound in Great Britain by Clays Ltd, Elcograf S.p.A.

Headline's policy is to use papers that are natural, renewable and recyclable products
and made from wood grown in well-managed forests and other controlled sources.
The logging and manufacturing processes are expected to conform to
the environmental regulations of the country of origin.

HEADLINE PUBLISHING GROUP
An Hachette UK Company
Carmelite House
50 Victoria Embankment
London EC4Y 0DZ

www.headline.co.uk
www.hachette.co.uk

To God, in whom, by whom, for whom and through whom I am.

For my daughters, Olaitan, Lola and Lara.

In honour of my ancestors, who paved the way.

*In loving memory of my father, whose words remind me
'In my country, I'm a first-class citizen'.*

CONTENTS

INTRODUCTION
MY SAY. MY FREEDOM.

'Arguably one of the most toxic voices in Britain's race relations debate, Dr Shola Mos-Shogbamimu . . .'

Telegraph, 16 June 2020[*]

I am Black British and an African from the roots of my hair to the soles of my feet. I state this with pride yet it is not lost on me that my proud heritage and identity are always in conflict with the deepening realisation that there is an unwritten narrative of what the Black identity is, which directly encroaches on my freedom to be me. ***This is why I resist.***

> 'I stand on the shoulders of greatness
> As my Ancestors before me
> I will not be silenced
> I will not be silent
> If you come for me
> I will come for you
> This is why I resist'
>
> Dr Shola Mos-Shogbamimu

---

* *Telegraph*, https://www.telegraph.co.uk/politics/2020/06/16/munira-mirza-bigoted-lefts-worst-nightmare/.

In the words of Bishop T. D. Jakes, 'If you know who you are, then you know who you are not. If you don't know who you are, somebody can ascribe any identity unto you and you will morph into whatever they want you to be." Well, I know who I am and believe that the philosophy of ascribing characteristics of dehumanising inferiority to Black people, in order to serve White supremacy, has existed for far too long. There is nothing superior about being White, and any notion of superiority is actually an inferiority complex. It must be unequivocally and resoundingly rejected. The contrived Black identity is not who we are and must not be ascribed to us any longer. I am personally tired of being force-fed negative tropes as my character. I know who I am not. *This is why I resist.*

It is the twenty-first century and racism is, without a doubt, another form of slavery, but one without visible chains. The Black identity has long been misrepresented, commoditised, marginalised and dehumanised due to a narrative that feeds the inferiority complex of White supremacy and White privilege. In my view, there is no freedom without rights and no rights without the freedom to exercise those rights. Freedom is a struggle. Black people are still fighting for freedom and rights. The freedom to be our authentic selves and the right to be judged by the content of our character and not the colour of our skin, as envisioned by Martin Luther King Jr's 1963 'I Have A Dream' speech.[†] So, regardless of whether we are *African, African American, Afro-Caribbean, Afro-Latin American, Afro-Arab, Afro-Asian, Afro-Chinese, Black Jews or Bi-racial of Black heritage,* the Black identity is plagued by generational White supremacy and White privilege that feeds and enables the racism,

---

* Bishop T. D. Jakes, 'Believe', December 2016, https://youtu.be/VmaePa6MoI4.
† Martin Luther King Jr's 'I Have A Dream' speech delivered during the March on Washington for Jobs and Freedom, 28 August 1963.

racial bigotry, racial prejudice and racial discrimination that shapes our lived experiences. Every space we occupy in the political, economic and socio-cultural sphere evidences our continued struggle for freedom. Be it in the workplace, at schools, on the street or in the echelons of power, the Black identity is on a collision course of resistance and defiance against pervasive and negative racial stereotypes. As well as resistance against White privilege, White silence, and denial of our lived experiences. From our skin colour, texture and style of hair, sexuality and temperament, body shape and form, abilities and skills to opportunities and outcomes, every Black person, old and young, schooled or not, able or disabled, rich or poor, faces the stigma of the contrived Black identity and the denial that our lived experiences exist. It is time to take back the narrative.

To readers looking for a dispassionate piece of writing or words sugar-coated to make you feel comfortable, this book is not it. The power of my resistance is fuelled by my passion, pride, anger, frustration, joy and authenticity. My accomplishments, as a Black woman, are not proof that racism does not exist but evidence of God's grace and the sacrifices of giants before me, including my parents, who paved the way.

Yes, I use 'White people' as a race colour specifier on the same terms that 'Black people' has been used to refer to people of African descent for centuries. I do not make the rules created by White nations to establish supremacy over those they considered inferior. But I will apply it in its colloquial terms to drive home the points on race, racism and race inclusion. Additionally, I do so because this is about the treatment of some by others based on the colour of their skin – 'White' and 'Black' is absolutely appropriate. So, if you are White, reading this book and offended, because it reads like '*all White people are the same*', get ready to be very uncomfortable. Take the time to ask yourself why you are so offended and perhaps the understanding you seek might come through. It is not my view that all White people are the same, but I will not be picking my words 'so as not to offend'. On the other hand, if you are White and understand from reading this book that there are layered nuances when I refer to 'White people', for example that there is a general context of Whiteness that can apply to all White people, such as White privilege and the weaponisation of Whiteness, and you also understand that certain acts committed by some White people do not necessarily apply to you – thank you for being so refreshingly honest and not requiring to be educated on this point. My resistance is my truth and, if it resonates with you, then I encourage you to resist with me. It is time to raise *your* voice as a White ally.

If you are Black or of another Ethnic Minority reading this book, I recognise we are not a monolith of one singular thought and that we may have similar or dissimilar nuances of experiences in our common struggle against the racism perpetuated against us. Many of us are done with being lumped together as BAME (Black, Asian and Minority Ethnic groups), as it has empowered the practice of institutional racism to ignore the struggles of respective groups by advancing the issue of one group above the rest. This differential treatment is simply more racism and imposes on us the indignity of being treated as a tick-box block. Yet we do have a common struggle. As I write in 2020, a year that has forced us to have the hard conversations about race, racism and race inclusion, that common struggle is evident, but my focus for this book has to be on the Black identity and the struggle of Black people against institutional racism. You may draw from it strength and solidarity or you may disagree with it; nevertheless, if my resistance resonates with you, then I encourage you to resist with me. It is time to give voice to *your* voice.

This book is the hard conversation we must have, and social media is the new battleground for points of views that epitomise the hard conversations on race, racism and race inclusion. Any social media posts referred to in this book are purely for analysis and/or as a point of reflection of how far we have come as a society, which is not very far at all. This book is my response to these hard and ongoing conversations happening in real time. Opinions drawn from social media help to frame the contexts of these hard conversations as well as project the mindset of society. Twitter is awash with contributions to this ongoing hard conversation on race, racism and race inclusion. I have referred throughout to tweets from individuals with significant followings and therefore the potential to influence large numbers of people with just a few words and tweets, as well as from other individuals that reflect differing views on the subject matter. Some tweets I have selected demonstrate how easily words are taken up as short-hand for entrenched views and shut out nuanced discussion. For the purposes of this book, I have chosen to focus the nuances of these conversations on Britain and America only. However, the resistance against the contrived Black identity equally applies to other countries, including France, Portugal, Spain and Belgium, all of which also have a legacy of slavery, colonialism and institutional racism.

This Is Why I Resist is a declaration that the Black identity will no longer be defined by a prejudiced mindset steeped in institutional racism that enforces White supremacy. A declaration that the Black identity won't be defined by the false claim that White people are 'creating spaces' for Black people, which in turn imposes an expectation we should be grateful to them for those spaces. The truth is those spaces were never theirs to control, command or claim in the first place. These were always *our* spaces, *our* lives, *our* opportunities and *ours* to control, command and claim. This book is an unfettered call to action to revolutionise the narrative around the Black identity. It will unequivocally and unapologetically address issues pertaining to it and posit an authentic approach to resistance. It is time for White people to face their history with slavery and racism, the legacy which continues to dehumanise Black people today. This is what Black people deal with every day.

This is why I resist.

'We do not fight the ignorant but the ignorance.'
Resurrection: Ertuğrul (Diriliş: Ertuğrul),
Netflix, Season 5

1

DOES WHITE PRIVILEGE WHITEWASH RACISM?

'Racism is a blight on the human conscience. The idea that any people can be inferior to another, to the point where those who consider themselves superior define and treat the rest as sub-human, denies the humanity even of those who elevate themselves to the status of gods.'*

Former President of South Africa, Nelson Mandela

The question of racism is no longer about what racism is but about how it manifests itself in the understanding of White people. White privilege whitewashes racism and whitewashing is the act, intentionally or not, of covering up, glossing over and/or excusing racism. There are two fundamental truths about racism. First, it is not the job of Black people and Ethnic Minorities to educate White people on racism perpetuated by White people. White people must educate themselves on the racism they perpetuate. Secondly, not all White people are racists. Some are, but *all* White people have and enjoy White privilege. This White privilege is what enables and enforces

---

* Nelson Mandela's address to the UK's Joint Houses of Parliament, 11 July 1996.

White supremacy. The furore from my TV interviews on ITV's *This Morning* and *Good Morning Britain*, when I stipulated that the UK is institutionally racist, and that racist attacks against Meghan Markle are whitewashed by White privilege, attests to this. The interviews sparked both public outrage and consensus in January 2020, as these tweets from a cross-section of views demonstrate:

> **Piers Morgan** ✔ @piersmorgan Jan 18 2020
>
> Don't tell me Shola... by criticising a shameless piece of work who's caused Harry to quit his country & family, am I being RACIST again?

> **James Jordan** ✔ @The_JamesJordan Jan 13 2020
>
> This black woman on This Morning talking about Harry and Megan is racist against "WHITE" people.
>
> FACT!!!
>
> #ThisMorning

> **Lisa Moorish** ✔ @LisaMoorish Jan 14 2020
>
> What's interesting is a load of white people, who have NEVER, or rarely experienced racism towards them, in a world dominated by right wing white supremacist racists, telling people of colour the things they know are racist, aren't racist at all. Please fuck off.

It was clear that 'White privilege' was a concept misunderstood by some because of the word 'privilege', which I will explain further in this chapter, but my comments definitely triggered White supremacy, hate and racist bigotry. There were also voices from different races and ethnicities, including White allies, who understood what I was trying to convey about White privilege and racism. They, in turn, tried to educate others, only to be piled onto with abuse for their efforts. The dissenting voices were the loudest and continued to grow in an attempt to silence me, but they only succeeded in proving my point. Racism is not an opinion and Black people's lived experience of it is not an argument up for debate. To understand why and how White privilege whitewashes racist behaviour and acts, and how it dehumanises the Black identity, we must first deconstruct Racism and White privilege.

A BRIEF DECONSTRUCTION OF RACISM

To begin with, racism is only perpetuated by White people and cannot be pigeon-holed into a neat box. It is far more complex and nuanced than just hate against a person because of the colour of their skin, so I have broken it down into three parts for ease of understanding. Each part jointly and severally underpins institutional racism. This means each part is equally responsible for racism perpetuated by White people, which has a deeply nuanced and layered history. This is why narratives of Ethnic Minorities, particularly Black people, being racist to White people have no substantive comparative basis or truth.

Part 1: Racism is a power construct created by White nations for the benefit of White people.

Racism is the belief that one's race is superior to another race and the imposition of that belief through an act, thought or words of racial prejudice, hate and discrimination. There is nothing unconscious about racism. The term 'race' is in itself a social construct designed to justify colonialism and imperialism because of the perceived superiority of White nations. Racism is the direct result of the transatlantic slave trade from the fifteenth century to the nineteenth century. The slave trade was the foundation of the American, European and industrial capitalism that created and boosted an international financial system. About twelve million Africans are estimated to have been forcibly kidnapped, enslaved and transported to Europe and the Americas. In return for African slaves to the Americas, sugar, cotton, coffee and tobacco went to Europe. Africa was impoverished and depopulated by the exploitation of its human and natural resources while Europe and America prospered with capital growth.

Part 2: Racism is a power construct fuelled by an unparalleled economic and political structure controlled by White nations to dehumanise, marginalise, commoditise, misrepresent and criminalise the Black identity for the benefit of White people.

The slave trade became the bedrock of the British economy. Beginning in the 1750s, Britain industrialised with cotton production as its major British industry, exporting manufactured goods and then importing slave products, such as sugar. Businesses were created with profits from the slave trade, as were businesses to supply goods and services to slave traders. Financial, commercial, legal and insurance institutions were established to underpin, underwrite and reinforce the transatlantic slave trade. White British people experienced economic, social and political positions of power over non-White people on the premise of superiority of race, knowing these positions of power could only be made possible by the blood, sweat, misery and death of African slaves.

While slavery has historically existed in societies across the world, the unique and damning feature of the transatlantic slave trade is that this slavery was purely racial and, most importantly, permanent. Africans were chattel bargained as property, and the status of the enslaved was inherited from generation to generation, all of which served the prosperity of White nations to the detriment of the African continent. Some argue the transatlantic slave trade was justified because slavery existed in some African societies. This is an ignorant justification to suggest and no comparison to the reality. The transatlantic slave trade was very different from servitude, where war captives, debtors or criminals might serve for a designated period of time in some African societies. This was not permanent nor did it cause them to lose their ancestral roots and be forcibly displaced for generations. The unequal power structure created by the exploitation of the African continent through slavery also created the conditions for colonial conquest following the abolishment of the transatlantic slave trade in 1808. More so, it created a toxic environment of racism that perpetuated an idea of the inferiority of Black people and the supremacy of White people. All of this to justify the continued exploitation of Africa and its people, which reflects the unequal power structures that exist between Africa, Europe and America today. It begs the question: where would Europe and America be today without Africa? White supremacy and racism not only survived the transatlantic slave trade, and the era of colonialism and imperialism, but became deeply rooted as racism institutionalised in the fabric of Western society, which in turn created the structural inequalities imposed on Black people.

Let this sink in.

It means that the Black identity was (and is) defined, framed and *dehumanised* by racism – a false notion that Black people are inferior to White people. This means the past, present and future of a Black person is *marginalised* to insignificance by the economic and political power structure of White supremacy. The hopes, potential, opportunities and abilities of the Black identity are *commoditised* for the prosperity of White people to the detriment of Black people. The *misrepresentation* of the Black identity through negative stereotypes today is similar to historical references to Black people as 'savage', 'mentally inferior', 'monkey-like in appearance' and/or of the 'Dark Continent'. All these references are used to justify treatment of them as less than human. The *criminalisation* of the Black identity is rooted in the perceived threat of Black people, to de-victimise them and condone racial violence against them.

Part 3: White privilege is a by-product of racism – an advantage solely based on being White and not predicated on socio-economic status, class or heritage.

The contrived Black identity arguably lives on in the mindset of some White people today and is evidenced in subtle or overt ways. Rather than reject this inhumane, unjust and unequal treatment of Black people, some White people are oblivious to it; others would argue freedom of speech as their defence; while perpetrators of racism justify their actions as their right. Some would even go as far as arguing that racism no longer exists and what would objectively be considered racist is called anything but racist. This includes, for example, referring to racist acts, behaviour or language as 'unfortunate' or to downplay its impact. This set of reactions is not a new phenomenon. We know why it exists and how it thrives. It is called White Privilege.

Be in no doubt that the transatlantic slavery of Africans was racial genocide and racial exploitation. It distorted Africa's economic growth as a continent making it wholly reliant on its colonial masters, who were exploiting it. It displaced millions of Africans, with many dying on the way to new lands and at the hands of ruthless White slave masters upon destination. And not only were Africa's mineral and human resources exploited, but it was strategically cut up to continue to feed the capitalist ambitions of White nations. The abolishment of slavery wasn't the end, as it was replaced with the colonisation of African countries. The untold number of attacks and the destruction of African people and communities who fought against the illegal occupancy of colonial masters is conveniently erased from British Empire history. That was genocide too. Do not think for one second that Africans did not put up a fight. To give but one example, Ologbosere, of Benin Kingdom, which is now in modern-day southern Nigeria, fought the British invasion following the Benin Expedition of 1897, in which one of the oldest and most highly developed African kingdoms was ransacked and destroyed by British forces. Ologbosere led the rebellion and resistance against Britain's unlawful invasion for two years before being caught and hanged in 1899 by British forces.

The denial of White privilege is an ugly truth that distorts the hard fact that this advantage was bought and paid for at the cost of Black lives and liberty. Those who deny White privilege exists know, even if only subconsciously, that their denial is a lie.

WHITE PRIVILEGE IS FACT NOT FICTION

Does the existence of racism mean all White people are racists? No. Does it mean, if you have White privilege, then *you* are racist? No. What it does mean is that all White people have White privilege and their perception of racism is clouded by that White privilege. Racism is not a matter of opinion but of experience. I would like to believe that no White person is born a racist but rather that racism is taught explicitly and/or covertly through societal norms of devaluing, dehumanising and discrediting Black people. I also know for a fact that no Black person is born knowing racism until they experience it. The experiences of many Black children racially abused for the first time, having to ask their parents for its meaning, and their confusion, hurt and often shame as to what could be wrong with the colour of their skin, attests to this. It is a privilege for a White child to never experience such shame, rejection and abuse because of the colour of their skin. White privilege is often misunderstood to be associated with wealth and class, but this is not the case. It is simply another form of privilege that confers an advantage in a different capacity. It is privilege based solely on the colour of White skin. It is the lived experience of every White person, regardless of their socio-economic background, education, wealth or class to benefit from implicit and explicit advantages in society in comparison to Black people and other Ethnic Minorities because of the colour of their skin. White privilege is not a matter of opinion but of experience.

The advantage of this privilege means White people will always be insulated by a media biased towards them, will never experience police racial brutality, will never deal with violent stereotypes associated with their race, will never experience workplace discrimination based on their race, and will never have their lived experiences denied or treated with suspicion. Fundamentally, in contrast to the Black identity, White privilege ensures that White people are not dehumanised, marginalised, commoditised, misrepresented and criminalised for the benefit of a perceived 'superior' race. Furthermore, there is an unparalleled economic and political power structure in place to support, reinforce and justify White privilege. The same power structure that underpins racism against Black people and the contrived Black identity fabricated for White supremacy. White privilege does not mean you have never struggled, grown up on a council estate or the projects, worked seventy hours a week, been homeless or on welfare benefits, or any other circumstance you wish to use to describe a lower economic status or class. It has absolutely nothing to do with that. It means your struggle has never been caused, amplified and structurally imposed on you because of the colour of your skin. A Black person in the same circumstances of economic status or class is subject to overt/covert racism and prejudice that worsen their struggle, which a White person will never experience because they are White.

White privilege is also a demonstration of how you cannot recognise and understand what you don't experience. Today we find White people (not all) often demand for racism to be proven to them – they place an unreasonable burden on Black people to explain it to them and propose solutions, all of which are then rejected as false or inconvenient to the White people's way of life. The denial of the lived experiences of racism by Black people happens from generation to generation. It is mentally, emotionally and physically exhausting for Black people.

When I challenged ITV *This Morning* co-host Phillip Schofield on why he was asking me for examples of racism against Meghan Markle when it is plain for all to see, his response was that he had not personally seen anything racist against her. Was I surprised? No.

But I had to then explain to him what racism looks like through the lens of White privilege:

> 'White privilege whitewashes racist and inflammatory lan-
> guage as unconscious bias, it perpetuates the bigotry of
> intolerant White people as ignorance, it defends and protects
> their private views once spoken as "misspeak", and then cam-
> ouflages racist behaviour as "error of judgement", which is
> exemplified by Danny Baker.'*

Centuries of derogatory and racist language, for example, linking the Black race to monkeys, apes, chimpanzees et al has been the lived experience of Black and Bi-racial communities. As explained earlier in this chapter, this racist behaviour goes as far back as the slave-trade era and today continues to exist under the politically correct term 'unconscious bias'. It is racist. In my view, there is no such thing as unconscious bias. Bias is consciously or sub-consciously expressed and just waiting for the right circumstances to trigger it. Intent is not a prerequisite to establish racial bias. The recipient suffers the same impact.

When ex-BBC Radio 5 live host Danny Baker posted a tweet depicting the baby son of the Duke and Duchess of Sussex as a chimpanzee, he insisted he wasn't racist. A man of intellect, exposure and influence such as this broadcaster (then sixty-one years old) claimed not to realise the connotations of his tweet. Instead he said: 'sincere apologies for the stupid unthinking gag pic earlier. Was supposed to be joke about Royals vs circus animals in posh clothes but interpreted as about monkeys & race, so rightly deleted.' He was actually surprised by the outrage, and referred to

---

* *This Morning*, 13 January 2020, https://m.youtube.com/watch?v=Yn3DEC79FIk.

those offended by the post as having 'diseased minds', saying it was an 'unconscious ridiculous tweet'. But this tweet was a racist act, and even the words used to express his non-apology are White privilege personified. As was the arrogance he displayed in attacking those he offended, and the notion his words could be explained away as royals versus circus animals when the tweet was captioned 'Royal baby leaves hospital'.

This is a privileged White man who claimed his lack of intent to cause racist offence should absolve him from what is objectively racist. Those who supported Danny Baker argued he lacked motive to incite racial hatred and sympathised with him because, in their opinion, he is a good broadcaster. They are basically saying that being a good broadcaster makes him incapable of being racist. Absolutely ridiculous. This standard of accountability is another product of White privilege that is notably never extended to Black people. Black people are perceived and judged by negative stereotypes endlessly, their actions and language continually scrutinised and, more often than not, seen to fall short of standards set by White people. There is never a question of allowing them the privilege of 'lack of motive' to determine whether or not they are guilty of an offensive act. They are simply guilty until proven innocent.

Let's also consider British historian David Starkey, one of the popular historians in the UK who made headlines in July, 2020 for racist remarks about slavery and Black people. He said:

'Slavery was not genocide, otherwise there wouldn't be so many damn blacks in Africa or in Britain, would there? An awful lot of them survived.'*

---

* Interviewed by Darren Grimes, https://m.youtube.com/watch?v=RpQYkmh1UtU.

His comments were not only repulsive and objectionable but outright racist. It is the literal equivalent of saying the Holocaust was not a genocide because some Jews survived it. His audacity to attempt to rewrite the history of transatlantic slavery and its use to fuel globalisation and capitalism for White nations is literally White privilege on steroids. And referring to 'damn Blacks', with such confidence there would be no consequences, as if Black people are roaches infesting Africa and Britain, exemplified and demonstrated his racist views of Black people. Particularly at a time of global #BlackLivesMatter protests, his racist comments caused nationwide outrage and led to consequences he could not have foreseen. Not surprisingly, however, social media was awash with dissenting and concurring views on whether or not his comments were a sackable offence.

David Schneider ✔ @davidschneider Jul 2 2020

> Never mind the ignorance about genocide, that "damn blacks" isn't just a shocking indictment of Starkey. It shows a confidence that you can say that because every time you have done in the past the people you're with nod along in agreement.

Toby Young ✔ @toadmeister Jul 2 2020

> If virtually everything and everyone in Britain is racist – its history, its museums, its monuments and statues, its universities, its criminal justice system, its Government, etc. – then why should we cancel David Starkey for being racist? Isn't he just like everyone else?

Sajid Javid ✔ @sajidjavid Jul 2 2020

> We are the most successful multi-racial democracy in the
> world and have much to be proud of. But David Starkey's
> racist comments ("so many damn blacks") are a reminder of
> the appalling views that still exist.

Given the severe backlash, David Starkey unsurprisingly did a 360-degree turn on his 'damn blacks' comment and gave a public apology for speaking 'with awful clumsiness' on his slavery comment.[*] Note how he does not take responsibility for his racist act? He refers to his comment as 'clumsy' rather than racist. Like Danny Baker, his apology is a whitewash of racism and only provoked further outrage, because, in his words, he had 'paid a heavy price for one offensive word with the loss of every distinction and honour acquired in a long career'. This is what he is sorry for – his loss, disgrace and shame. He shamelessly failed to read the room and thought his deliberately inflammatory comments about Black people and slavery would cause outrage without consequences. Yes, he clearly thrives on controversy and has probably often sought to create controversies to maintain some sort of relevance with his base of conservative and alt-right audience, but that's no defence. He also responds with the classic 'I am not a racist' explanation to assure us his comments do not reflect his views or practice of race inclusion:

> 'I have lived and worked happily and without conflict in multi-cultural London for almost 50 years and I spent much of the podcast discussing bi-culturalism as a key to the success of Britain's multicultural society.'[†]

---

[*] BBC News, https://www.bbc.co.uk/news/entertainment-arts-53308061.

[†] Ibid.

This is outdated gaslighting, pure and simple – it is the equivalent of 'I have a Black friend, Black spouse/partner, my kids are
Bi-racial etc'. It is getting so old. Racists should come up with a more
creative response to deny racism, like – don't be racist! When I read
his statement about 'living and working happily' in multicultural
London, what I hear him saying is that non-Whites are okay as long
as *they* don't create conflict and *they* know their place. Professing
to be in sync with Britain's multicultural society is very much at
odds with him saying 'Black Lives Matter protests, following the
death of George Floyd, had been characterised by "violence", "victimhood" and the "deranged" pulling down of statues.' You can't
divorce the two. Claiming it is a 'misunderstanding of my words'
is literally passing the buck of responsibility to those he offended.
Apparently, it is *our* fault not *his* for not understanding he did not
mean the exact words he used against Black people about racial
genocide and racial exploitation of slavery. Interestingly enough,
there are those who argue that the offensive word in his comment
is the word 'damn', and that was clumsy not racist. Once again,
as with Danny Baker, we see racist language, as used by Starkey,
whitewashed as 'mis-speak.'

Starkey goes further, though, in order to preach the need for free
speech, as he fears his 'blundering use of language' will stop proper
debate. Note he still refuses to acknowledge his comments as racist.
Now he adjectivizes it with 'blundering', as though that captures
the heinousness of his racist comment or the devastating impact of
his White privilege to the disadvantage of Black people at a globally
sensitive time, with so many calling for #BlackLivesMatter.

White privilege has staying power because of the ongoing existence of institutional racism, which creates systemic intersecting
inequalities against Black people. The structural intersection of
multiple forms of inequalities enables a consistent, destructive and

toxic co-existence of inequalities in the lives of Black people. This is not only evidenced in the interaction between Black and White individuals but also in the interaction between White and Black nations. The power structure that birthed White privilege manifests structural inequality. This is the legacy of the transatlantic slave trade and the subsequent colonialism and imperialism used to legalise the exploitation of entire nations.

Within the context of racism and discrimination, White privilege enables a vicious cycle that permits White people to get away with language and actions that are atrociously inflammatory and derogatory, consequently causing the potentially irreparable damage of mistrust and inequality in our multi-cultural and multiracial society. Abuse of White privilege in the wrong hands incites racial hatred, leads to the death of Black people (as you find in cases of police brutality), causes unfair treatment and discrimination of Black people and Ethnic Minorities in the workplace, schools and communities, and visibly rewards racist behaviour of White people whose advancement is not impeded in the least. I would go as far as to say that White privilege is the indivisible inheritance of every White person from birth, whether they know it or not, the same way every Black person from birth is ascribed a contrived Black identity solely to feed the White supremacy that gives White people their inherited White privilege.

The connotation of White privilege as a 'woke' and 'leftist' propaganda by actor Laurence Fox on BBC *Question Time* in January 2020 is the latest line of defence from some White people perpetuating the denial of centuries of White privilege, which has protected them from the suspicion, bias, prejudice and dehumanising social status endured by Black people and Ethnic Minorities purely based on the colour of their skin. Politicising White Privilege as leftist is deliberately inflammatory, in order to distract from the issue of the inequalities underpinning it, and labelling anti-racists as 'anti-White' and 'woke' is deliberate, so as to discredit campaigners calling out racism. Basically, White privilege entitles White people to 'police' Black people's lived experiences of racism. Some politicians even play it safe by not publicly acknowledging racism or empathising with Black people, both of which are seen to be political liabilities.

In October 2020, when Equalities Minister Kemi Badenoch, a Conservative Black British MP, made the headlines with a categorical statement in the House of Commons that 'schools which teach pupils "White privilege" is an uncontested fact are breaking the law', she was effectively denying White privilege exists, censoring teaching racial inequality as illegal, and politicising the lived experiences of Black people as if it were up for debate whether Black people experience racism as a direct result of the advantages of White privilege that White people benefit from. There is no doubt that her words, particularly as a Black politician, legitimised views that discredit and delegitimise anti-racism efforts for social justice and race equality. For many in the Black community, her actions were particularly reprehensible because they help further the cause of White supremacy and, as an Equalities Minister, it was a clear demonstration that she is not an ally to the resistance against race inequality.

I personally could not give a flying flamingo about the defensiveness and sensitivity of some White people to the truth that their wilful ignorance of racism is aided and abetted by their White privilege. It is White privilege when White people try to impose their definition of racism on Black people. In my view, it was the height of White privileged petulance for Laurence Fox to say on

---

* Jessica Murray, 'Teaching white privilege as uncontested fact is illegal, minister says', *Guardian*, 20 October 2020, https://www.theguardian.com/world/2020/oct/20/teaching-white-privilege-is-a-fact-breaks-the-law-minister-says.

BBC *Question Time* that 'racism should only be called out when it's obvious'* or Piers Morgan's adamant refusal to accept the lived experiences of Black and Ethnic Minority guests (including me) during debates about racist press coverage of Meghan Markle in January 2020 on ITV's *Good Morning Britain* when he said 'I'm not accepting that just because I am white, I can't see racism when I see it.'† White privilege defines racism along the lines of burning crosses or using the N-word. This is as obvious as it gets for some White people. However, do bear in mind how many years/centuries it took them to even accept burning crosses and the N-word are racist. So not only do Black people and Ethnic Minorities get oppressed by racism, some White people have the audacity to define, curtail and police what our lived experience of racism is while denying they have White privilege that enables and benefits from institutional racism. ***This is why I resist.***

CONCLUDING THOUGHTS . . .

Silence is not an option, it is complicity. Ambivalence, apathy and the constant state of obliviousness are intolerable and complicit. Racism and White privilege are institutionally engrained in the fabric of British and American White societies. It runs deep in our history and culture, and is singularly responsible for the economic and financial wealth of both nations. Regardless of whether you're African, African American, Afro-Caribbean, Afro-Latin American

---

* *Metro*, 17 January 2020, https://metro.co.uk/2020/01/17/laurence-fox-claims-racist-called-white-privileged-male-bored-race-card-question-time-12073306/?ito=cbshare.

† *Metro*, 15 January 2020, https://metro.co.uk/2020/01/15/piers-morgan-claims-black-people-calling-fat-white-gammon-racist-12059901/?ito=cbshare.

or Bi-racial of Black heritage, there comes a day of rude awak-ening when single and/or multiple occurrences open up your understanding of how your Black identity is perceived and mis-construed. Not because there's a failing in the content of your character but because of an endemic system of racism that thrives on dehumanising, marginalising, commoditising, misrepresenting and criminalising the Black identity for the benefit of a perceived 'superior' White race. Before we were taught what resistance was, we were the resistance.

Echoes of the plight of our ancestors are within us, like a memory chip in our bloodstream. You know instinctively something isn't right. This sixth sense is not imagined, it is survival. Often, we may not have the words to articulate what our minds are processing but we eventually see the pattern of racism and White privilege as it courses through our timeline both offline and online. Society is con-ditioned to see certain forms of White privilege as mild or harmless when the impact is devastating, mentally, emotionally, physically and, inevitably, fatally. White privilege excuses, denies and glosses over racist, prejudiced and discriminatory acts or language every day – this is the lived experience of both Black and White people. This is a non-exhaustive list of what White people can do that Black people in the same circumstances would be vilified or even killed for if the roles were reversed:

Stephen Lawrence in the UK, aged nineteen, murdered in a racially motivated attack by four white boys, teaches us that the ordinary act of waiting for a bus is not safe for Black people. The Macpherson public inquiry report into the Lawrence murder then, many years later, found the police guilty of institutional racism. **Ahmaud Arbery** in the US, aged twenty-five, shot dead by two white men while jogging in his neighbourhood, teaches us that vigilante White America uses the stereotype of Black people as criminals to justify modern-day lynching of Black men, even when jogging.

Meanwhile, in 2019, football commentator **Gary Neville** was applauded for speaking out against racism after Antonio Rudiger was racially abused by a Spurs fan, while Grime star **Stormzy** was attacked by the media and on social media for saying that there is racism in the UK. Both men should be applauded for speaking out against racism, but White privilege gives Neville a cloak of perceived legitimacy that Stormzy does not have. Instead, Stormzy is labelled with the contrived Black identity that perceives young Black men as social delinquents and 'ungrateful'.

A broken criminal justice system teaches us that White privilege will protect a White mother from the full force of the law while disproportionately criminalising a Black mother for the same or similar crime. Wealthy White American mother and actress **Felicity Huffman** was sentenced to fourteen days in prison but did only eleven days for paying for her daughter's college entrance exams to be fixed, while single African American mother **Kelley Williams-Bolar** was sentenced to five years, which was suspended, and then imprisoned for ten days for using her father's address to enable her kids to get into better public schools. Homeless African American mother **Tanya McDowell** was convicted for 'stealing an education' and sentenced to twelve years in prison with seven years suspended for sending her son to school in a different district from the district she lived in as a homeless person. In my opinion, surely Felicity Huffman bribing the proctor to fix her daughter's entrance papers, which her daughter could have simply sat herself, is the definition of 'stealing an education'?

Neither Kelley Williams-Bolar nor Tanya McDowell's use of a different address justified either their prosecution or conviction for giving their children access to a better public-school education. Their punishment was racially discriminatory, disproportionate and outrageous.

A 2018 survey on everyday bias in Britain revealed that Ethnic Minorities are 'three times as likely to have been thrown out of or denied entrance to a restaurant, bar or club' and that 43% of Ethnic Minorities had been overlooked for a work promotion.* In a 2019 survey of race relations in America, 65% of those who responded said expressing racist or racially insensitive views is more common since Trump was elected president, and 52% say being Black hurts their ability to get ahead.† The disproportionate use of force against Black people is also discriminatory – in Britain, the Police 'Use of Force' statistics revealed that Black people experienced a disproportionate use of force in England and Wales by the police, while White people are less likely to be subjected to use of firearms or tasers.‡ A White person would never need to change his or her name to get jobs because their name is Black-sounding, or be asked 'Where are you really from originally?' The credibility of a White person is more likely to be trusted because of their skin colour than a Black person's credibility, while a Black person is more likely to be presumed guilty for a crime or wrongdoing than a White person purely based

---

* Robert Booth and Aamna Mohdin, 'Bias in Britain', *Guardian*, 2 December 2018.
† Juliana Menasce Horowitz, Anna Brown and Kiana Cox, 'Race in America 2019', Pew Research Center, 9 April 2019.
‡ Police use of force statistics, England and Wales: April 2017 to March 2018 – available online , published 13 December 2018, https://www.gov.uk/government/statistics/police-use-of-force-statistics-england-and-wales-april-2017-to-march-2018.

on race. And Black children and students do not have the privilege of learning about their own race and diverse ethnicities in schools, where White historical figures are overrepresented by a whitewashed curriculum and educational system. The list goes on.

We must resist the inequality normalised by White supremacy because White privilege *is* inequality. It normalises racist behaviour and language. It feeds the contrived Black identity, which is fuelled by racism. To be clear, this resistance is a collective 'We', which includes other Ethnic Minorities and White allies. This is a clarion call to speak up, show up and stand up for Black people as a collective resistance to end institutional racism and dismantle White supremacy.

2

DOES 'REVERSE RACISM' EXIST?

'I am not a racist in any form whatsoever. I don't believe in any form of racism. I don't believe in any form of discrimination or segregation.'*

Civil rights activist, Malcolm X

The favourite form of abuse online trolls use against me on social media and via email is to call me a 'racist'. The basis of this reverse use of 'racist' on me is their claim that I stir up hate against White people by calling out racism entrenched institutionally and perpetuated by White people, and that my campaigns as an activist to fight injustice and inequality are anti-White. Like Malcom X, Martin Luther King Jr and others before me, I am neither racist nor anti-White. What I am is anti-racist and unapologetic in my condemnation of systemic structural inequalities and institutional racism. Time and time again I am told to go back where I came from, told to be grateful, and told I owe everything to Britain, and this is the mild version of the abuse thrown my way.

To the whataboutism of 'racism against White people', I can tell you categorically that it does NOT exist. Those claiming reverse racism exists must live in a dystopia – an imagined world like the

---

* Malcolm X speaking at the Ford Auditorium in Detroit, 14 February 1965.

one created by former Children's Laureate Malorie Blackman in *Noughts and Crosses*, where societal hierarchies are reversed and those with Black skin have the power and wealth, while those with White skin are powerless and oppressed by racism. The novelist James Baldwin goes further to explain why the notion of reverse racism has no substance or merit, because the power to enforce racism is not reversed:

> 'It must be remembered that in those great days I was considered to be an "integrationist" – this was never, quite, my own idea of myself – and Malcolm was considered to be a "racist in reverse." This formulation, in terms of power – and power is the arena in which racism is acted out – means absolutely nothing: it may even be described as a cowardly formulation. The powerless, by definition, can never be "racists," for they can never make the world pay for what they feel or fear except by the suicidal endeavor which makes them fanatics or revolutionaries, or both.'*

There is no equal playing field or role reversal in the actors and perpetrators of racism, as White people would have us believe. Racism is not an all-embracing word that includes non-Whites as perpetrators. White people cannot claim racism is equally perpetrated by both White and Black people while still claiming racial superiority. Baldwin reminds us of the divide and rule tactic of colonial masters when he points out language used by White people to describe him and Malcom in a way to cause division, though both their goals were the same in calling out the oppression of

---

* James Baldwin, *No Name in the Street*, Dial Press, 1972.

Black America and demanding the liberation of Black people in all aspects of life.

DECONSTRUCTING 'REVERSE RACISM'

Reverse racism is imagined or perceived by White people as hate expressed against them because of the colour of their skin. If, indeed, racism is reversed, then surely Parts 1 to 3 of 'A brief deconstruction of racism', as set out in the previous chapter, should also be evidenced and present in reverse racism? I would therefore like to test the concept of reverse racism on all three parts.

Part 1: Racism is a power construct created by White nations for the benefit of White people.

We know racism is the premise upon which the transatlantic slave trade was justified and that inhumane oppression and subjugation were imposed on Black people. By definition, in Chapter One, racism is the belief that one's race is superior to another race and the imposition of that belief through an act, thought or words of prejudice, hate and discrimination. There is historical and present-day evidence to demonstrate racism was designed and perpetuated against Black people as an inferior race on the sole basis that White people are superior.

Where is the evidence of this in reverse? When were White people as a race oppressed and subjugated by Black people? That has never happened. Black people have never imposed any superiority of race as an expression of hate against White people. We have always been clear we are equal to the White race, not inferior. Racism was neither created by Black people nor does it benefit them in any way. The concept of reverse racism therefore fails the first test.

Part 2: Racism is powered by an unparalleled economic and political structure controlled by White people to dehumanise, marginalise, commoditise, misrepresent and criminalise the Black identity.

We know that racism is enforced by an unequal power structure, centuries in the making, that still exists today, an economic, social and political power structure that negatively impacts the quality of life and choice of Black people. Equally, this power structure thrives on the perceived racial superiority of White people in order to dehumanise, marginalise, commoditise, misrepresent and criminalise Black people. Where is the evidence of such a power structure utilised by Black people against White people in this concept of reverse racism? There is no such evidence. Economic, social and political institutions within White nations and globally between nations are not structurally controlled or commanded by Black people or Black nations. Black people cannot and do not utilise power to negatively impact the quality of life and choices of White people as an entire race. Reverse racism therefore fails the second test.

Part 3: White privilege is a by-product of racism – an advantage solely based on being White and not predicated on socio-economic status, class or heritage.

We know White privilege is an advantage of colour to White people as a race, based on the notion of White supremacy. This is evidenced in the daily lived experiences of White people. It means a Black person in the same circumstances as a White person would be treated unequally because they are Black. Chapter One discusses the insulation, protection, leverage and advantage White privilege bestows on White people over and above Black people. No matter how educated, wealthy or well-connected a Black person is, White supremacy judges them by the colour of their skin not the content of their character. White privilege protects White people from ever experiencing such indignity, always giving them the benefit of the doubt as to the content of their character, something which is never afforded to Black people. Where is the evidence of an equivalent 'Black privilege' in the concept of reverse racism? There is no such evidence. As an example, the fabric of British and American societies is entrenched with the supremacy of colour so that the word of a White man or woman is taken as gospel truth over that of a Black man or woman. Black people have no control or command of the fabric of these societies to create an advantage of colour for Black people to produce a privilege with such pervasive dexterity. Reverse racism therefore fails the third test.

So, we can conclude that White people do not experience racism. As a construct based on the superiority of race underpinned by an unparalleled power structure, the by-product of which gives them a unique privilege solely based on the colour of their skin, White people do not experience racism from Black people. If, for one day, White people ever experienced the racism they constructed and imposed on Black people, they would end racism. The discomfort some White people feel when racism is challenged is profoundly telling when they attack Black and Ethnic Minorities as racist or

accuse them of stirring up anti-White sentiment. White supremacists, the far right and the alt-right thrive in the United Kingdom and
the United States on the false claim of reverse racism. They hark back
to a time these nations were 'Great', as a single White race. This is
delusional, because the only racism perpetrated is by them and their
targets are Black people and Ethnic Minorities. Accusations of anti-
White and reverse racism are deliberate tools of White supremacists
and the alt-right to distract from the fight against institutional racism
experienced by Black people and Ethnic Minorities. There is no such
thing as 'reverse antisemitism' or 'reverse Islamophobia' or 'reverse
homophobia', etc., so why are Black people accused of the heinous
inhumanity perpetuated against them? As an example, when Jews
or Muslims speak strongly and boldly against hate crimes and the
hate speech used against them, they are never accused of 'reverse
antisemitism' or 'reverse Islamophobia'. Bear in mind that the horrific atrocities of the holocaust were perpetrated and perpetuated
by White people against Jews. It would be wrong to appropriate
the antisemitic or Islamophobic experience as the oppression of
the actual perpetrators of the hate. Yet some White people try to
appropriate the oppression of institutional racism inflicted on Black
people as their own by claiming a false equivalence, and then blame
Black people for it. This is another great example of White privilege.
This is our lived experience.

RACISM IS NOT A CATCH-ALL PHRASE

Racism against Black people must not be appropriated as a catch-all
phrase for all forms of hate or discrimination against other races or
ethnicities. Just as reverse racism is an attempt to falsely claim White
people are subjected to the racism they subject Black people to, I

find that the term racism is now being used as a catch-all phrase for other expressions of hate.

When the godfather of grime music, Richard Cowie Jr (aka Wiley), a British grime music artist, went on a tirade of antisemitic abuse on Twitter in July 2020, it triggered a strong backlash and condemnation, and rightly so. People demanded that social media platforms be more decisive in dealing with antisemitism. However, some people made the point of saying antisemitism is racism. It most definitely is not. These are two distinct expressions of hate and it does a disservice to those oppressed by both to treat them as one and the same. Here's why. There is a common struggle that is shared between Jewish people and Black people against the oppression of antisemitism and racism. Martin Luther King Jr aptly captures this sentiment:

'My people were brought to America in chains. Your people were driven here to escape the chains fashioned for them in Europe. Our unity is born of our common struggle for centuries, not only to rid ourselves of bondage, but to make oppression of any people by others an impossibility.'*

This sense of a common struggle reflects the similarities of the experiences of hate, prejudice and bigotry based on false philosophies against Jews and Black people. Nevertheless, it does not make both expressions of hate the same. I can only share my humble opinion on why they are not the same and that both should be accorded the same level of energy, advocacy and resistance to eradicate the menace both expressions of hate represent and cause.

---

* Address given by Martin Luther King Jr at the 1958 American Jewish Committee convention.

Antisemitism is not racism. It punches upwards against Jews by falsely claiming Jews are a power construct that they are not and maligns them with century-old tropes blaming them for heinous acts or behaviours that are NOT true. Racism against Black people punches downwards, representing a power construct of White supremacy inflicted on Black people based on perceived inferiority of racial skin colour. Antisemitism is not about inferiority of racial skin colour. Anyone can be antisemitic – White, Black and Brown people can be antisemitic towards Jews if they believe and/ or act on antisemitism. Not everyone can be racist. Anyone can be anti-Black, but that is different from racism. Anti-Black is the opposition or hostility to Black people or 'perceived Blackness'. It does not require a power construct like racism to support it, neither does it deny Black people an equal value of life and liberty, as systemic racism does. Anti-Black is divisible from, and co-exists with, systemic racism. In my opinion, anti-Black is propagated mostly at a micro level by individuals, unlike systemic racism, which is indivisible and permeates through institutions and individuals alike at macro and micro levels of society. A person can be anti-Black but not manifest systemic racism. As an example, other Ethnic Minorities, such as Asians, can be anti-Black, but there is no such thing as Asian or Brown supremacy to give it longevity, nor did they create a power structure of inequality against Black people, nor impose a privilege of superiority of race. This is not systemic racism.

Black people experience racism from White people regardless of the socio-economic status, faith or class of the White person because the power construct of White supremacy manifests systemic racism to deny Black people an equal value of life and liberty for the benefit of White people. Jews are also denied an equal value of life and liberty because of the fear and hate against them, falsely based on a notion that they are a power construct, among other falsehoods. Some people accuse Jews of having Jewish privilege. There is no such thing as Jewish privilege, just as Black privilege does not exist. Both racism and antisemitism are grounded in hate, but with unique and distinct originating bases. Bear in mind that there is only one race, i.e. the human race, and that 'race' as we know it today is a social construct. White Jews benefit from White privilege but are not oppressed or subjugated by White supremacy, while Black Jews experience both antisemitism and racism as well as being subjugated and oppressed by White supremacy. But let's take a look at how the injustices of antisemitism and racism intersect.

Treating antisemitism as racist denies Black Jews the justice they deserve for each distinct expression of hate they experience. The nuances of antisemitism and racism are lost and does a disservice to the magnitude of pain, dehumanisation and suffering both cause. When antisemitism is called racist, it is centring Whiteness and ignoring Black Jews, who experience both distinct expressions of hate. If you end antisemitism today, it will not end racism. If you end racism today, it will not end antisemitism. Ergo, antisemitism is not racism. They co-exist, and intersect, but they are not the same thing. Racism is not a catch-all phrase. Antisemitism is not a catch-all phrase either.

For the same reasons, Islamophobia is also not racism or a catch-all phrase. It is a distinct expression of hate based on religious prejudice and bigotry that is anti-Muslim and anti-Islam. Muslims are people from all genders, all races, all sexualities, creeds and socio-economic backgrounds, etc. from all over the world. They experience targeted expressions of hate towards Islam, their Muslimness or perceived Muslimness. Islamophobia transcends race. People of other faiths convert to Islam and vice versa, as with Judaism,

Christianity and other religions. As an example, White Muslims may experience Islamophobia but not racism. When Black Muslims experience Islamophobia, they are more often than not also experiencing racism, because of their Black identity being perceived as an inferior race. Muslims are not a race – they are from all races. A Muslim is a follower of the faith of Islam. It is important not to diminish the intersecting inequalities and resulting injustices Muslims with different backgrounds will experience by treating Islamophobia as racist. Both are distinct expressions of hate that should be afforded the justice each deserve. I speak out against antisemitism, Islamophobia *and* racism. I use the same level of advocacy, anger and resistance against each one and want justice for each. That is not possible if we treat them as the same. And the people who suffer from treating multiple intersecting expressions of hate the same in Britain and America are Ethnic Minorities, particularly Black people.

There's no hierarchy in hate and I strongly oppose the misappropriation of 'racism'. Islamophobia, antisemitism and racism are heinous expressions of hate that must be resisted with the same level of force, advocacy and resistance to eradicate them. A light must be shined on how they intersect to afford the oppressed visible and unequivocal justice. Bear in mind that the origin of racism is steeped in the transatlantic slave trade of Black people and a power construct to feed the appetites of colonialism and imperialism. Expressions of hate have many faces and names, e.g. antisemitism, homophobia, anti-gypsism, etc., but only racism was historically used to define and describe the racial discrimination, prejudice and racial bias against Black people. Racism is not just hate of a person based on the colour of their skin but the unparalleled economic and political power structure rooted in White supremacy that underpins and supports the systemic oppression of racism against Black people and other Ethnic Minorities by White people. There is no competition between racism and other expressions of hate. They are equally heinous crimes against humanity. Common struggles and similarities exist between these different expressions of hate but that does not make them the same.

DO WHITE PEOPLE EXPERIENCE RACISM?

NO. White people do NOT experience racism. White people can experience prejudice, but this is not racism. Every race and ethnicity face prejudice and discrimination at some level, but this is not racism. The cause and effect of racism and prejudice are very different. White people are also subjected to bias, but this is not racism and cannot be substituted for racism at the hands of a so-called 'inferior race'. Prejudice is a set of preconceived assumptions or stereotypes that express intolerance and bias against a person for a number of reasons, including race, faith, disability, sexuality, etc., but there is no systemic power structure to support it or give it longevity. It tends to be demonstrated by individuals as opposed to vast institutions that control the social, economic and political structure of a society. Prejudice and bigotry against White people are not acceptable or justified. However, calling out racism, prejudice and bigotry perpetuated by White people is neither prejudice nor racism against them. It is literally speaking truth to power. In my opinion, this famous quote by American author and poet Scott Woods succinctly illustrates the dilemma White people have with how racism manifests in their understanding:

> 'The problem is that white people see racism as conscious hate, when racism is bigger than that. [. . .] Racism is an insidious cultural disease. It is so insidious that it doesn't care if you are a white person who likes black people; it's still going to find

a way to infect how you deal with people who don't look like
you. Yes, racism looks like hate, but hate is just one manifestation. Privilege is another. Access is another. Ignorance is
another. Apathy is another. And so on. So while I agree with
people who say no one is born racist, it remains a powerful
system that we're immediately born into. It's like being born
into air: you take it in as soon as you breathe. It's not a cold
that you can get over. There is no anti-racist certification class.
It's a set of socioeconomic traps and cultural values that are
fired up every time we interact with the world. It is a thing
you have to keep scooping out of the boat of your life to keep
from drowning in it.'*

None of the elements outlined in this quote are present against
White people for any semblance of reverse racism to exist. The
socioeconomic traps are set against Black people not the other way
round. This is part of the power structure that fuels institutional
racism and works solely for the benefit of White people and is reproduced by them. The struggle to end the injustice and inequalities
of institutional racism has long been fought because those who *can*
change it *won't*.

WHITE LIVES MATTER

When I am faced with racism, prejudice and White privilege trying
to misappropriate the struggle and oppression of the Black identity as
'White Liberation' or 'White Lives Matter', my DNA explodes with

---

* Scott Woods, 3 January 2014, https://scottwoodsmakeslists.wordpress.com/
2014/01/03/5-things-no-one-is-actually-saying-about-ani-difranco-or-plantations/.

the knowledge that we have seen this before. 'White Liberation' and 'White Lives Matter' are the same justifications used to oppress Black people for centuries. I refuse for this to happen on my watch, so I resist. 'White Liberation' is the face of White supremacy. This concept of liberation is obsessed with the false equivalence of racism perpetuated against Black people and Ethnic Minorities as victimisation of White people. The cause and effect of this obsessive push for White liberation is evidenced in the divisive election of Donald Trump as President of the United States of America, and vocally expressed in the division, xenophobia and racism evidenced in the UK Brexit elections. White people who follow the 'White Liberation' agenda fail to recognise their own racism and possess the uncanny ability to make themselves the victim in the construct of racism that they, as White people, have created to oppress Black people.

White Lives Matter is a racist response to the Black Lives Matter movement and, in essence, a hate group dedicated to the preservation and supremacy of the White race. They claim that White people are the victims of racial genocide and that the integrity of the White way of life is damaged by mixed relationships between White people and Black people or Jews. It claims White America is targeted by issues such as 'illegal immigration, healthcare, housing, welfare, employment, education, social security, our children, our veterans and active military etc'. In response to the civil rights Black Lives Matter movement, the co-founder of White Lives Matter reportedly said 'what happens to blacks in this country at the hand of law enforcement is none of our concern [...] other than to prepare to restore order and rebuild our neighborhoods taking back our lands one community at a time.'* Watching the protests led by

---

* Rebecca Barnette, White Lives Matter co-founder, 16 July 2016, https://www.splcenter.org/fighting-hate/extremist-files/group/white-lives-matter.

certain White people to 'liberate' the State of Michigan, USA, from the Social Distancing order set by Governor Gretchen Whitmer prompted me to post a tweet reproduced below. The lack of fear as they stepped up to police, shouted in their faces, disrupted the peace, etc., just magnified the unequal treatment of law enforcement in regards to Black protesters, who would have been beaten, gassed, arrested or, worse, shot dead if they had behaved similarly.

Dr Shola Mos-Shogbamimu @SholaMos1 4 May 2020

The False equivalence of 'White Liberation'

'Imagined' loss of liberty
No fear of being gassed, beaten or shot
Endangering Lives at Will
Bloody White Privilege on Steroids

No Police in fear of their lives
No weapons drawn
Even A Cop yawns
Bloody White Privilege on Steroids

White supremacy is on a collision course with the Black Identity. Not the contrived identity that perceives Black people as inferior to White people, but the Black Identity that is the rise of the Black consciousness: knowing who we are, speaking in the truth of our authenticity; and challenging the socio-economic and political barriers that have imposed an unequal and unjust regression of our human rights. Everything racists fear. As long as the progress of Black people is dependent on how it impacts the comfort and way of life of White people, the friction of this collision course between White supremacy and Black identity will continue.

When British actor Laurence Fox said to Rachel Boyle, an audience member on BBC *Question Time*, 'to call me a white privileged male is to be racist', this is a great example of the use of reverse racism and the false equivalence to White supremacy. He then went further to tweet Martin Luther King Jr's 'I have a Dream Speech' as the principle he lives by in life. A clear contradiction of his denial of White privilege, which was proven by accusing a woman of colour of being a racist because she called him a White privileged male. The appropriation of Martin Luther King Jr's 'I Have A Dream' speech by Laurence Fox to feed, what seems to me, to be his toxic self-justifying ineptitude is nothing short of White Privilege personified. The audacity to misuse powerful words that held the hopes of millions from a history steeped in slavery, suffering and the emancipation of Black people, was, to many minds, including mine, reprehensible. But this is what White privilege can get away with. Furthermore, I have no doubt that if Martin Luther King Jr was to call Laurence Fox out as a White privileged male, just as Rachel Boyle did on BBC *Question Time*, Dr King would be subjected to the indignity of being called a racist too.

This false sense of anti-White discrimination and prejudice is also centred around diversity and inclusion. I think some White people are struggling with the new reality that they have to share power, liberty and equality with a race their way of life is predicated on denying an equal value of life and liberty to. There is no equivalence of racism suffered by Black people being imposed on White people. According to a 2011 study, White Americans see racism as a zero-sum game, which they are now losing. White respondents perceived that there is a decline in anti-Black bias in comparison to a sharp increase in anti-White bias.* However, the

---

* M. Norton and S. Sommers, 'Whites See Racism as Zero Sum Game that they are now losing', *Perspectives on Psychological Science* 6(3) 215–218, 2011.

reality is proven to be the opposite, as evidenced by real-life experiments undertaken in 2017, which included but were not limited to testing White and Black American respondents seeking housing or employment. Results of the experiments showed racism as the cause of disparity, with Blacks discriminated in favour of Whites by a large margin.* Some White people, particularly White men, fear that workplace diversity programs are discriminatory and make them an undesirable classification, while some feel that they get passed over for promotion in favour of Black and Ethnic Minorities. In 2019, Microsoft pro-diversity efforts were challenged internally by some staff as discriminatory against White men. In 2017, Google fired an employee, James Damore, who complained that Google's diversity efforts were ideological and discriminated against White men. These are all otherwise known as conservative viewpoints.

These conservative viewpoints are hailed by the alt-right as shutting down political correctness on diversity and inclusion. They see policies of affirmative action to increase Black and Ethnic Minority representation as discrimination against White people. Anti-White discrimination is also perceived to exist in the irrational fear among some White people that acceptance of multi-culturalism from different ethnicities dilutes the 'White' way of life, its norms and values. As much as I welcome and engage in debate with opposing views, I resist any notion that we, Black people and Ethnic Minorities, should bear the brunt of the irrational fear of White people.

---

* L. Quilliana, D. Pager, O. Hexela, and A. H. Midtbøen, 'Meta-analysis of field experiments shows no change in racial discrimination in hiring over time', *PNAS* 10870–10875, 10 October 2017, vol. 114. no. 41.

COMPLACENCY IS COMPLICITY

I reiterate that silence is not an option. Complacency is complicity. Our Black ancestors were not silent. Their back-breaking work as either enslaved people on plantations or enslaved as colonised nations, bearing terrible loss of life and liberty, putting their heads down to fight another day, and overcoming overwhelming odds, was not silence. This was survival so that descendants like me can today do what they could not do, say what they could not say and go where they could not go. History dictates that the culture of institutional racism (which is the 'White way of life') means that the rationalisation and tolerance of moderate White people makes them complicit. History also teaches us that White people do what is best for White people. Complacency in the status quo or obliviousness to how their privilege and way of life negatively impacts the quality of life and choice of Black people *is* complicity.

Martin Luther King Jr referred to this as the polite 'racism' of White moderates. Note the difference between White moderates and advocates of White Liberation. White moderates are White people who see themselves as progressive and embrace racial diversity, liberal immigration policies, acknowledge the oppression of their history, etc. and are more or less aware of their White privilege and the inequality to Black people, but this 1963 quote by Martin Luther King Jr is as relevant today as it was then:

'I must confess that over the past few years I have been gravely disappointed with the white moderate. I have almost reached the regrettable conclusion that the Negro's great stumbling block in his stride toward freedom is not the White Citizens Council of the Ku Klux Klanner, but the white moderate, who is more devoted to "order" than to justice; who prefers a negative peace which is the absence of tension to a positive peace which is the presence of justice; who constantly says "I agree with you in the goal you seek, but I cannot agree with your methods of direct action""*

I could not agree more with Martin Luther King Jr, I personally find that White apathy and complacency are the nails that drive institutional racism home. This famous quote, attributed to Edmund Burke, comes to mind: 'the only thing necessary for the triumph of evil is for good men to do nothing.' To my mind, White people who are apathetic to institutional racism are just as racist as the White people who are openly racist. I would go as far as also calling these 'White moderates' cowards, as succinctly described by Abraham Lincoln, who said: 'to sin by silence when there should be protest makes cowards of men.'

CONCLUDING THOUGHTS . . .

This is why all voices are needed to work in solidarity in raising awareness on root causes of institutional racism and why the White moderate's complicity is damaging to Black people. It also goes to show that reverse racism does not exist.

In July 2020, Harry and Meghan, the Duke and Duchess of Sussex, spoke out against institutional racism and the need to come to terms with the uncomfortable legacy of the colonial past of the Commonwealth. Harry and Meghan then caused more controversy during Black History month, in October 2020, when they drew attention to the need to end structural racism in Britain. In their

---

* Martin Luther King Jr, 'Letter From Birmingham Jail', 16 April 1963.

words, 'for as long as structural racism exists, there will be generations of young people of colour who do not start their lives with
the same equality of opportunity as their white peers.'* This led to
a deluge of dissent from those who viewed the comments as disrespectful to the Queen, or interfering with the current affairs of the
day to do with institutional racism in the UK, or were outraged
that a member of the royal realm would acknowledge structural
racism exists in Britain. While concurring views agree that Britain
today can't be divorced from its colonial past, clearly the focus of
the dissenters was to discredit the Sussexes, because they consider
their departure from senior royal duties as a betrayal of the country.
This is, of course, utter nonsense. The Sussexes did not 'betray'
Britain by stepping down from royal duties. For example, the faux
outrage against Harry and Meghan over the uncomfortable truth of
Britain's past with the Commonwealth gives much-needed insight
into how pride in Britain among the dissenting voices is predicated on the exploitation of its legacy of slavery and colonialism of
Africa. The Commonwealth of nations has a legacy of colonisation
with those members that were anglophone countries colonised by
Britain. Whatever benefit these 'independent' anglophone countries
have from this union is unequal in the power and benefit the United
Kingdom gets from them. Some of the economic ties link to existing
arrangements pre-dating the independence of these nations.

In the present-day fight to end institutional racism, Britain's
shameful past in its colonial history and profiting from millions of
Africans stolen, enslaved, killed and dehumanised for centuries is

---

* 'The Duke and Duchess of Sussex: Our BHM Next Gen trailblazers list will
champion Black Britons' triumphs', *Evening Standard*, 1 October 2020, https://
www.standard.co.uk/comment/comment/bhm-next-gen-trailblazers-harry-
meghan-a4560916.html.

important to understand. Black Lives Matter has been our clarion call from the moment the first African was sold off the shores of the African continent. As such, the #BlackLivesMatter movement is a continuation of a centuries-old freedom struggle. The ethos and essence of this movement was at the core of the Civil Rights movement, the abolition of slavery, independence from colonialism, and the eradication of apartheid. But please note I speak of the movement and not the BLM organisation of the same name, an organisation of which I am not privy. How can we begin to move forward if we don't acknowledge the mistakes and impact of Britain's colonial past?

The truth is we cannot. Failure to address the past in order to build a new legacy for the future is what partly breeds the false equivalence of reverse racism. It would be going down the rabbit hole to think that White people who claim Black people are racist to them are simply ignorant of their history and of its legacy in the present day. This is the twenty-first century and I am done with those who are consciously oblivious to racism and their part in it, and inevitably enable White supremacy as a result. Reverse racism is an oxymoron.

3

CAN WE BREATHE, PLEASE?

'Freedom is never voluntarily given by the oppressor; it must be demanded by the oppressed. For years now I have heard the word "Wait!" It rings in the ear of every Negro with piercing familiarity. This "Wait" has almost always meant "Never." We must come to see that [. . .] "justice too long delayed is justice denied."'*

Civil Rights activist, Martin Luther King Jr

I write this chapter knowing the exhaustion of Black people in having to repeatedly relive experiences of racism when sharing what we come up against. I recognise our indignation at the demand to 'justify' our oppression as racist while absorbing the pain of the immediate dismissal and denial of our lived experience in order to silence us. I write this chapter knowing that the journey to action 'justice too long delayed' is systematically frustrated, and that fighting 'justice denied' is constantly having to go back to the drawing board to relive that systemic frustration and revisit the injustice. It is traumatic and triggering. The trauma is a vicious cycle of experiencing the violation and desecration of the Black identity time and

---

* Martin Luther King Jr, 'Letter From Birmingham Jail', 16 April 1963, http://okra.stanford.edu/transcription/document_images/undecided/630416-019.pdf.

time again without recourse to immediate justice. We experience a lack of care for our psychological, physical and mental well-being, and are shown utter contempt for the impact this trauma has on our quality of life and choice. *We can't breathe.*

Our ability to breathe is visibly constricted in plain sight. The structural systems that choke us are rooted in a culture of White supremacy that shapes the economic, political and social systems that reinforce the legacy of slavery and colonisation. The systems, laws, policies and processes built to establish fairness, access to justice, financial independence, stop social injustice, etc. also suffocate the very people they are meant to protect. The atrocities Black people endure are in plain sight and despite the existence of discrimination laws, equality legislation and democratic process reveal a reality of structural intersecting inequalities that can be compared to a vicious cycle where the predator ruthlessly exploits its prey despite laws of protection to protect it. *We can't breathe.*

Black people don't control the power construct to reform existing systems steeped in inequality nor do we control the power to build new foundations that break away from the structural systems that have choked us. Racism and White privilege are weaponised against us daily, in overt and covert ways, regardless of socio-economic status or class. Incremental changes in laws or having representation from Black, Asian and Ethnic Minority communities in certain positions of power does not change the fact that countries like the United Kingdom and United States are historically and presently institutionally racist to Black people. If the greatest trick the devil pulled was convincing the world he did not exist, then the second greatest trick he orchestrated in the world is the denial of the existence of racism as the modern form of slavery. *We can't breathe.*

We live with the unavoidable truth that race is a key determinant of intergenerational upward and downward social mobility. For every milestone, we are told to 'wait'. That our time will come. The implication, often voiced, is clear that we should be grateful, and so we are admonished like a wayward child for gross impatience. We are reminded of a time when 'social mobility' was non-existent for people like us, so we must take heart and rejoice at the incremental changes that have led to 'an opportunity' for mobility. But the reality is very different. This opportunity is neither equal nor does it equate to equal outcomes. The façade of 'opportunity' has long lost its potency as we come to realise it is not created for our benefit but rather centred on how much opportunity White society deems acceptable at any given time. *We can't breathe.*

Yet when these burning injustices are raised and our experiences shared, we are castigated for playing the victim and racialised in victimhood. Our strength in surviving and thriving against the odds is neither recognised nor celebrated. In fact, any form of success Black people achieve is credited to a 'tolerant and least racist society', while any disadvantage we face is blamed on our 'inability to pull ourselves up by the bootstraps'. The consciousness of constantly turning the other cheek, erosion of our dignity and persistent badgering of the Black identity as second-class and inferior is cast aside as inconvenient truths. We endure all this while the power construct of institutional racism continues to cause ongoing social and economic oppression. When we show defiance against these burning injustices, we are stereotyped as troublemakers, race baiters, militant and anti-White. *We can't breathe.*

You. Yes, you, White siblings, some of you, refuse to dismantle White supremacy, argue ignorantly about your White privilege and play dumb about unlearning overt and covert racist behaviour you have been exposed to. Some White people even claim they are unaware of how they benefit from and/or reproduce racism but still refuse to educate themselves about it. They pass all their responsibility to unpick and unlearn to Black people. You want us to do the heavy work of unpicking and teaching and then transmit it to you in bite-sized chunks at your convenience, comfort and leisure. You expect us to do all this while dealing with the onslaught of visible and invisible individual barriers of racism and carrying the collective weight of experiences our Black identity bears. Our load is enough. Nevertheless, the expectation is on Black people to be patient, as though we are not human beings capable of exhaustion. Some White people even refuse to recognise their own fragility or dig deep into the source of their discomfort, guilt and rage when the subject of racism is raised. Yet even in this, their defensiveness, faux outrage and gaslighting is blamed on us. *We can't breathe.*

The caucasity of tone policing Black people when we talk about the impact and continued legacy of slavery and colonisation in the present day is solely to silence us. Demanding we talk about racial inequality in a positive way that only focuses on making White people comfortable is similar to the cruel expectation forced on plantation slaves to appear happy serving their masters. Demanding us to be focused on what we should be 'grateful for' rather than what we are 'equally entitled to' goes to show ongoing efforts to deny an equal value of life and liberty to Black people. Taking offense and expressing White outrage is classic White supremacy used against Black people. *We can't breathe.*

TAKE YOUR KNEE OFF OUR NECKS

'If you are calling for an end to this unrest [. . .] but you are not calling for the end to the conditions that created the unrest, you are a hypocrite.'*

US Representative Alexandria Ocasio-Cortez

'8 minutes, 46 seconds' will go down in history as the trigger that globally revolutionised hard conversations about race, racism and race inclusion in the twenty-first century. The killing of an African American man, George Floyd, by White police officer Derek Chauvin on 25 May 2020 triggered global protests against racism and raised awareness about persistent and heinous police brutality against Black people. More so, this was particularly significant in the United States and Britain, where racial inequality is driven and incited by racially divisive political and economic motives.

George Floyd was arrested for allegedly using counterfeit money to buy cigarettes. In a graphic and distressing video taken by an onlooker, viewers see Floyd pinned face down to the ground, restrained and in handcuffs, with police officer Derek Chauvin's knee pressed down on his neck for 8 minutes, 46 seconds. Floyd's pleas that he can't breathe were ignored, and shouts from onlookers that he was no longer talking went ignored by all four police officers on the scene. Throughout, White police officer Derek Chauvin kept his knee forcefully down on the neck of George Floyd. It was a cold-blooded killing captured live on video and shared instantly to the world. No crime of counterfeit money is penalised by death under

---

* Samantha Michaels, 'Alexandria Ocasio-Cortez Speaks to Supporters About the Minneapolis Protests', *Mother Jones*, 30 May 2020, https://www.motherjones.com/politics/2020/05/alexandria-ocasio-cortez-minneapolis-protests-george-floyd/.

the law, yet this police officer effectively acted as judge and jury in wilfully and recklessly sentencing George Floyd to death. What was blatantly obvious was how safe, protected and untouchable Derek Chauvin felt in doing so. Not one of the other three police officers present stopped him or told him to ease off the pressure on George Floyd's neck or listened to the anguish of George Floyd and onlookers. The utter disregard and contempt for the life of this African American man by a White police officer gave new meaning to nuance. Not because police brutality is something new but because the ugliness and brutality of his killing opened the eyes of White people to the insidious presence of racism. George Floyd died not because of an alleged counterfeit $20 bank note but because he was a Black man accused of a crime. Yet some conversations around his death openly deny racism present in the circumstances of this visible killing. Social media was awash with both concurring and dissenting opinions on the issue, as in these tweets:

Anti-Social Distancing @GodsExperiment Jun 27 2020

| What about George Floyd's death was racist?

Gina Bontempo @FlorioGina Jun 8 2020

Two things can be true at once:

George Floyd's **death was** unjust and wrong.

Racist police brutality is not a systemic issue. In fact, if you were to make a list of the top 10 things devastating black communities today in America, police brutality wouldn't even make the list.

Tory Fibs @ToryFibs Jun 1 2020

> **George Floyd**'s **death** has just been declared a homicide in
> an independent autopsy after a state autopsy claimed his
> primary cause of **death was** an underlying health condition.
>
> Racism is most oftyen invisible to the naked eye. Botched
> paperwork is as **racist** as a knee on a neck.

These tweets reflect the mindset of some on both sides of the pond. Dissenting voices literally deem what is objectively racist as anything but 'racist' and require evidence to be provided to prove racism against Black people. Who died and made them judge and jury over our lived experiences? They look for any reason to not see racism and treat Black people's lived experience of racism as if it is up for debate. It most definitely is not. The video evidence of Floyd's death was not enough. They need a blow-by-blow explanation, which they will no doubt still reject. Though not all police are bad and not all White police officers are racist, there is no denying that there are White police who are bad and racist. Police brutality against Black people is rooted in racism. Evidently White privilege affords some White people the boldness to refute the evidence before their eyes and reject the lived experience of racism in Black lives. Racism which they have never experienced and will never experience. They demand proof of it for the sole purpose of denying racism exists.

SYMBOLISM OF THE WHITE KNEE ON THE BLACK NECK

I want to deconstruct what the White Knee on the Black Neck symbolises by breaking it down to two elements. The first element the

White Knee symbolises is *power*. Chauvin's knee represented a double-sided sword that could only be wielded by him and not Floyd. On one side of the sword is the power of the police institution, which represents the ultimate authority. It also has a history of protecting officers like Chauvin from prosecution in the event they commit a crime or misconduct. Please note that prosecution here has a double meaning. It does not mean he cannot be prosecuted in a court of law, but that any such prosecution would most likely lead to an acquittal. Inevitably, the prosecution is justice being window dressed with no actual justice given. This was demonstrated in the prosecution of the police officers in 1991 who brutally beat **Rodney King** more than fifty times with a baton (a 2-foot solid piece of aluminium) in Los Angeles; in the prosecution of the police officers who, in 1999, shot **Amadou Diallo** more than forty times and killed him – all of whom were acquitted; and, in 2015, the death of **Freddy Gray**, who suffered fatal injuries in police custody, which were likened to a car crash because his spinal cord was nearly severed, and where, of the six police officers charged, one was a mistrial, two were acquitted and charges were dropped against the others. This, among many other such cases from time immemorial onwards, have understandably led to zero trust from Black people in the criminal justice system.

On the other side of the sword is the power of White privilege, which can be seen as Chauvin wilfully wields his perceived White racial superiority over a Black man. This notion does not require intent to be achieved or accomplished. The visible manifestation of his knee on Floyd's neck was all that was needed to represent White racial superiority. Both these powers made Chauvin consciously and visibly powerful. The Black Neck represents no power. Not even Floyd's right as a citizen is recognised because the Black identity has long been criminalised so that all that is seen of this alleged suspect are the negative stereotypes associated with being Black. Even to the extent that the very police institution that should protect the Black Neck from harm is weaponised against it. Furthermore, there is no privilege for the Black Neck to draw from. The symbol of racial superiority is complete.

It is easy to think of the Knee and Neck purely in the context of the United States, but that would be ill-formed. Britain manifests the same racial superiority, often in plain sight, and more often than not under the guise of polite society and religion. A strong example is the Most Distinguished Order of Saint Michael and Saint George, one of the highest honours awarded by the Queen of England to those who render extraordinary or important non-military service in relation to Foreign and Commonwealth affairs. The symbol on the badge purportedly shows St Michael trampling on Satan. However, a closer look shows St Michael as a White man and Satan as a Black man. The symbolism of the White man trampling the neck of a Black man in this badge is evident and racist. More so is the fact that this reflected the mindset in 1818 when this order of chivalry was founded by King George IV, and undeniably still represents the underlying mindset of White supremacy in the United Kingdom during the reign of Queen Elizabeth today. Who says angels are White or that Satan is Black? Had it truly never occurred to anyone for over 200 years how offensive this is? While this does not mean the Queen herself is racist or that every head of British Government is racist, it does evidently demonstrate that Britain and its institutions are intrinsically and undeniably founded in the racist doctrine of White supremacy, which enables and enforces institutional racism. It shows how wilfully blind and complicit British society has been in keeping the status quo of White supremacy. This is because, consciously or sub-consciously, their way of life is predicated on the denial of an equal value of life and liberty for Black people. *This is why I resist.*

Institutional racism exists at every level of the British criminal justice system, from arrest to prosecution, and from conviction to sentencing. It is important to note that the police brutality which led to George Floyd's death is also prevalent in Britain. Evident in Britain is the same level of excessive use of force and prejudicial mindset that has a devastating impact on Black British communities, just as it does in America with African American communities. The main difference is that not as many of these incidents are captured on phone cameras in Britain as they are in America, or they are not as widely covered and reported by UK mainstream media. However, the tide is turning and more Black British people are realising that filming police brutality and discrimination is actually a form of protection against the police.

Those who posit that there is no police brutality in Britain or that Britain is 'less' racist compared to America, or that police brutality in Britain is somewhat justified, suffer from a severe case of selective amnesia or are ignorant of history. They conveniently forget or were never taught about the Broadwater Farm riots in 1985 that were triggered by the death of **Cynthia Jarret**, who died of heart failure widely believed to be a result of the police mistreatment she suffered at home, or about the 1993 murder of **Stephen Lawrence**, which, due to his mother Doreen Lawrence's relentless campaigning, led to the 1999 MacPherson inquiry, which found the police to be institutionally racist. According to a CNN survey conducted in June 2020, Black British are twice as likely as White British to say British police are institutionally racist, with 54% of Black respondents and 27% of White respondents confirming this.*

Conveniently, those in denial also forget the unjustifiable shooting of **Cherry Groce** in her home by a London Metropolitan Police officer, which sparked the Brixton Uprising of 1985. According to her young son, who had witnessed it, she had also said 'I can't breathe', just like George Floyd. What about **Joy Gardener**, who was killed in 1993 when police officers pinned her down to the ground, handcuffed her and gagged her with a 13-foot length of adhesive tape wrapped around her head? How can anyone conveniently forget **Sean Rigg**, who died in police custody in 2018 after being restrained by police officers for at least seven minutes, or **Rashan Charles**, who died in police custody in 2017, falsely suspected of swallowing a package of drugs, which was not true.† He was heavily restrained by the police, who forcibly searched his mouth using neck and throat holds, which led to Rashan choking to death. Or **Jimmy Mubenga**, who was unlawfully killed in 2010 on a plane on the Heathrow runway while being restrained by

---

* Richard Allen Greene, 'CNN poll shows what Black Britons have long known – from policing to politics, their country has failed them', CNN, 22 June 2020, https://edition.cnn.com/interactive/2020/06/europe/britain-racism-cnn-poll-gbr-intl/.

† Tom Powell, 'Rashan Charles death: Father-of-one did not swallow drugs before dying in police custody, watchdog reveals', *Evening Standard*, 2 August 2017, https://www.standard.co.uk/news/crime/rashan-charles-death-fatherofone-did-not-swallow-drugs-before-dying-police-custody-in-dalston-police-a3602671.html.

three immigration officers, and even though the inquest held Jimmy was killed unlawfully, all three officers were acquitted at trial for his death. **Sarah Reed**, meanwhile, was at the centre of a police brutality case in 2012 when police officer James Kiddie accused her of shoplifting. He was caught on CCTV grabbing her by the hair and dragging her across the floor, pressing on her neck and punching her multiple times in the head. **Sheku Bayoh** died in police custody in 2015, with up to six police officers restraining him, and with his hands and legs bound. His body was found to have twenty-three separate injuries from the police restraint. It is clear that the disproportionate and excessive use of force targeted against Black people by some police officers is unjustifiable. Every single person brutalised by the police is denied an equal value of life and liberty as a result of unjustifiable excessive use of force by the police. Their deaths and loss of liberty must not be in vain. Say. Their. Names. *We can't breathe.*

It almost beggars belief that with so many deaths recorded in police custody in England and Wales since 1990, no officers have been convicted for the deaths of Black people at the hands of police brutality as far as I am aware. According to the charity Inquest, there is irrefutable evidence of structural racism embedded in police practices and the disproportionality of the use of force against Black people is proof of this.[*] Inquest's analysis of Black, Asian and Ethnic Minority deaths further revealed that these deaths are 'disproportionate as a result of use of force or restraint by the police, raising serious questions of institutional racism as a contributory factor in their deaths'.[†] According to a BBC analysis in June 2020, Black

---

[*] Deborah Coles, 'The disproportionality in the use of force against black people adds to the irrefutable evidence of structural racism in policing practices', *Inquest*, 11 June 2020, https://www.inquest.org.uk/bame-deaths-in-police-custody.
[†] Ibid.

people are more than twice as likely to die in police custody than White people when you compare the percentage each group represents in the population to the percentage of their deaths in police custody.* *We can't breathe.*

The second element the White Knee on the Black Neck symbolises is *cause and effect*. John F. Kennedy's 1963 Civil Rights speech aptly captures the moral issue of institutional racism as it presents today, over fifty years later:

'but are we to say to the world, and much more importantly, to each other that this is the land of the free except for the Negroes; that we have no second-class citizens except Negroes; that we have no class or caste system, no ghettoes, no master race except with respect to Negroes?'†

Kennedy is addressing the treatment of Black people as inferior second-class citizens to White people and the trampling of their hard-worn rights in a predominantly White nation founded on the premise of the irrefutable truth that 'all men are created equal', as stated in the 1776 US Declaration of Independence. 'All men are created equal' was true in 1776 with Thomas Jefferson, when America declared its independence from Britain; true in 1963 with John F. Kennedy, addressing the Civil Rights movement; and true in 2020, when declaring Black Lives Matter following the death of George Floyd. But what is evident in each century represented by these years and in between is that though all men are created equal, they are not treated equally.

---

* Reality Check team, 'George Floyd death: How many black people die in police custody in England and Wales?', BBC, 3 June 2020, https://www.bbc.co.uk/news/52890363.

† John F. Kennedy speech, 'A Report to the American People on Civil Rights', 11 June 1963, https://m.youtube.com/watch?v=7BEhKgoA86U.

The Black skin is the common denominator in any considered reflection on how race operates in treating African Americans and Black British people as second-class citizens. The simple fact is that the Black skin is the underlying probable cause for every discrimination and racism experienced by African Americans and Black British. The cause is the fear, hate and suspicion of the melanin content of our skin. The indignation of being treated as inferior is not relegated to the archives of history when it is lived daily. It may take a different shape or form, but it is the same indignation just in a different century, different year and different day. The burden of being told you are not welcome, you don't fit, you're not good enough, being criminalised, facing threats of intimidation, fighting for your human dignity and equal outcomes can never be relegated to the archives of history when it is lived daily. All of which exist to oil the wheels of White supremacy.

Some White people literally try to gaslight us into thinking racism was a thing of the Civil Rights era in the desperate attempt to deny racism exists today. Pre-Civil Rights era, racism was readily identifiable in both America and Britain. For example, in the 1950s and 1960s, common daily experiences of Black British included being openly denied jobs and housing and being met with blatant and unequivocal signs that read 'No Blacks, No Dogs, No Irish'. The 1950s and 1960s is not history; it was yesterday. Likewise, it should not be lost on us that Jim Crow segregation laws did not end in America until as recently as 1965. Slavery ended in America in 1865, but it took one hundred years for all African Americans, not just those in the North, to exercise the right to vote in 1965. We are talking about roughly sixty years ago, which is still relatively our present and not some far-flung century in the past. Many Black British and African Americans who experienced this are still alive today.

The effect of institutional racism may not be as readily identifiable to the White consciousness today, but it still reverberates in the Black consciousness. While some White people expect racism to look like it did in the days of Jim Crow and the British 'No Blacks' signs, many Black people are dealing with the evolving shape of racism in all of its forms. All this under the glaring eye of laws already put in place to end discrimination and inequality. Common experiences of racial inequalities in employment, housing, income, promotion and workplace discrimination remains persistent. In both America and Britain, the 'war on crime' became dog-whistle for 'war on Blacks', premised on the contrived Black identity of White supremacy.

The British civil rights protests that strove to wrench the proverbial White knee off our British Black necks took place not that long ago in cities such as London, Manchester, Bristol and Birmingham. It goes to show that this has been a long and continuous struggle. There is nothing fictitious about a struggle to remove the shackles of the legacy of slavery or to find that what was abolished as slavery took a different form of oppression, disadvantage and denial of equal rights. The 1963 Colour Bar protests in Bristol, a former major slave port, led to a watershed moment as it tackled the open secret of excluding non-White workers, particularly Black people, from the transport industry. Yes, it was a milestone in achieving equality; however, Black people still experience race discrimination in employment today in 2020, even though race discrimination was banned in the UK in 1976. What was openly a colour bar in 1963 covertly exists today and manifests itself in the continued struggle for diverse representation in industry sectors, promotion or lack thereof of Black talent, and the still existing disadvantage of having a non-English sounding name when applying for jobs. So, still, *we can't breathe*.

We must also not forget that Parliament did not pass legislation on race relations until the passage of the Race Relations Acts in 1965. Again, the year 1965 is literally like yesterday and not some far-flung century deep in history. The Race Relations Act was largely due to the co-ordinated efforts and lobbying of the Campaign Against Race Discrimination from 1964 to 1967.* The centuries it took to get to this law shows that equality for Black Britons was not a priority and the fact that we are still battling for equality in comparison to White counterparts' evidences why Britain is relatively young in race equality. So, still, *we can't breathe*.

In America, Jim Crow laws evolved into the dog-whistle for 'war on drugs', which specifically targeted Black people with disproportionate sentencing and mass incarceration, among other things. Black people were made to fit the crime with the probable cause being the colour of our skin. President Nixon's former domestic policy chief, John Ehrlichman, aptly captures the cause and effect of the White Knee on the Black Neck in plain sight:

'We knew we couldn't make it illegal to be either against the war or black, but by getting the public to associate the hippies with marijuana and blacks with heroin. And then criminalizing both heavily, we could disrupt those communities. We could arrest their leaders, raid their homes, break up their meetings, and vilify them night after night on the evening news. Did we know we were lying about the drugs? Of course we did.'†

_____

* This organisation was inspired by Martin Luther King Jr's visit to London on his way to Stockholm to receive his Nobel Peace Prize.

† Tom LoBianco, 'Report: Aide says Nixon's war on drugs targeted blacks, hippies', CNN, 24 March 2016, https://edition.cnn.com/2016/03/23/politics/john-ehrlichman-richard-nixon-drug-war-blacks-hippie/index.html.

Using subtle terms with thinly veiled racial appeals to vilify Black people is one of the ways racism manifests today. Harry LeRoy 'Lee' Atwater, political consultant to US President Ronald Reagan, aptly explains how language is politicised to capitalise on racism against Black people by securing White votes on the basis of 'what is worse for Black people is good for White people':

'You start out in 1954 by saying, "Nigger, nigger, nigger." By 1968 you can't say "nigger" – that hurts you, backfires. So you say stuff like, uh, forced busing, states' rights, and all that stuff, and you're getting so abstract. Now, you're talking about cutting taxes, and all these things you're talking about are totally economic things and a by-product of them is, blacks get hurt worse than whites . . . "We want to cut this," is much more abstract than even the busing thing, uh, and a hell of a lot more abstract than "Nigger, nigger."'*

Can White people ever understand the challenge of a Black identity so dehumanised and marginalised? Would they be ready to swap places with us for even one day? Especially, when some appear to capitalise on and agree with the coded messages that Lee Atwater and John Ehrlichman describe, which is 'what is worse for Black people is good for White people'. This is the analogy of the White Knee on the Black Neck personified. The inevitable effect of the constant insidious and systemic suffocation of Black people is for the sole purpose of denying them an equal value of life and liberty for the benefit of White people. While some White people recognise this injustice and

---

* Rick Perlstein, 'Exclusive: Lee Atwater's 1981 Interview on the Southern Strategy', *The Nation*, 13 November 2012, https://www.thenation.com/article/archive/exclusive-lee-atwaters-infamous-1981-interview-southern-strategy/.

fight against it alongside Black people, other White people are either complicit in silence or vocally support this injustice. This is because their way of life is predicated on the denial of an equal value of life and liberty to Black people. *We can't breathe.*

The White Knee on the Black Neck is still widespread today, be it overtly or covertly manifested. However, because some White people expect racism to look the same as it did sixty years ago, they are either wilfully oblivious or deliberately failing to identify racism in its various forms today. In fact, a number of White people would argue there is no racism and that Black people today have the same opportunities as White people. They do not see racism as the cause and effect of African Americans and Black British experiencing inequality and disparities in employment, housing, income, etc. in comparison to their White counterparts. What we have achieved through civil rights protests and legislation in both America and Britain have led to incremental changes but do not change the fact that there is still much work to be done to achieve real parity in equality. Still, *we can't breathe*.

In his eulogy at George Floyd's funeral, American civil rights activist and Baptist minister Reverend Al Sharpton summed up the White Knee on the Black Neck powerfully:

'We are not fighting some disconnected incidents. We are fighting an institutional, systemic problem that has been allowed to permeate since we were brought to these shores and we are fighting wickedness in high places. [...] Oh, if you would have had any idea that all of us would react, you'd have took your knee off his neck. If you had any idea that everybody from those in the third ward to those in Hollywood would show up in Houston and Minneapolis, and in Fayette-ville, North Carolina, you'd have took your knee off his neck.

If you had any idea that preachers, white and black, was going to line up in a pandemic, when we're told the stay inside and we come out and march in the streets at the risk of our health, you'd have took your knee off his neck, because you thought his neck didn't mean nothing.'*

WEAPONISING WHITENESS

'Until the philosophy which holds one race superior and another inferior is finally and permanently discredited and abandoned – everywhere is war.'

Former Emperor of Ethiopia, Haile Selassie I [†]

Everyday racism is manifested when White people weaponise their Whiteness against Black people. This is another way the White Knee on the Black Neck is symbolised in the lived experiences of Black people. Weaponising Whiteness is literally the act of using White privilege as a weapon to reinforce White supremacy for either personal benefit or for maintaining the status quo of false superiority claimed by White society. Whiteness has long been an advantage Black people have long borne with to their detriment, which is undoubtedly why *we can't breathe*. It is not the complexion of being White that is the problem but the ramifications of White identity, which mask the prevailing sycophantic notion that being a White person makes you stronger, better, more deserving or capable than a Black person.

---

* Transcript of Reverend Al Sharpton's eulogy speech at George Floyd's funeral in Houston, 9 June 2020, https://www.rev.com/blog/transcripts/reverend-al-sharpton-george-floyd-funeral-eulogy-transcript-june-9.
† Haile Selassie I's address to the United Nations, 1963.

The genesis of weaponising Whiteness against Black people is deeply embedded in the legacy of slavery in the United States and Britain. Confronting the truth of this legacy means looking at such weaponisation purely on the basis of race. While some would argue that it is quite wrong to do so because that would dismiss and relegate all of our human qualities to irrelevance, I would argue that I do not make the rules. It cannot be right that White supremacy denigrates the Black identity and sums up all our human qualities as 'inferior' because of the colour of our skin but, when we confront them for weaponising their Whiteness against us as racist, we are accused of being anti-White. Sounds like hypocrisy and double standards for one rule to apply for them and another for us. Remember parts 1 to 3 of Chapter One on deconstructing what constitutes racism? Racism is a power construct created by White nations for the benefit of White people to deny Black people an equal value of life and liberty. White society made the rules, hence we cannot be blamed for applying the same standards to the ruthlessness of the impact of their false sense of racial superiority. Still unclear about what I mean? Let's take a look at some examples of weaponising Whiteness to give this some more context.

The privilege of calling the police on Black people for NOT breaking the law is at best an attempt to unjustly deny us our liberty and at worst a death sentence, given the undisputed excessive use of force resulting in police killings of and violence against Black people. It is hard to believe that there is any White person left in America or Britain who is unaware of the breakdown of trust between the police and Black communities unless that person was literally born yesterday. Knowing of or being wilfully oblivious to police brutality against Black people and wantonly disregarding the potential harm involving the police may cause to that Black life is racist. Why do they do this? It is borne out of fear. The fear of

Black people in White spaces. Not just being in White spaces but owning, thriving and even appearing to belong is enough to trigger weaponising White privilege to activate the police under the false claim of danger or threat to their life. Not taking responsibility for putting Black lives in danger of police brutality is unacceptable.

Just weeks after the unlawful killing of George Floyd, an employee at Wendy's Restaurant in Atlanta called the police on **Rayshard Brooks**, who was found asleep in his car in the Wendy's parking lot. The officers deployed their Taser on Brooks for allegedly resisting arrest as they tried to tackle him to the ground for failing a breathalyser test, and he grabbed one of the officer's Tasers and ran. Police officer Garret Rolfe dropped his own Taser, unholstered his handgun and shot at Brooks three times as he ran away. How can the circumstance of a young man asleep in a parking lot have escalated so quickly to excessive use of force by the police, killing him? It wouldn't have happened if he had been White under the exact same circumstances. *We can't breathe.*

STARBUCKS

In 2018, when two Black men, **Rashon Nelson** and **Donte Robinson**, did not order anything in a Starbucks in Philadelphia while waiting for a third friend to join them, Starbucks manager Holly Hylton called the police, claiming they were causing a disturbance and trespassing. This was subsequently found to be untrue and, in my opinion, turned out to be exactly what it looked like – racism. Holly Hylton weaponised her Whiteness because she felt these Black men fell short of a standard expected of the White space owned by Starbucks. Should Starbucks staff be doing this? *No.* Is it wrong? *Absolutely.*

White Starbucks customers would never experience this dehumanising treatment for doing the exact same thing. It exemplifies racial discrimination at an organisation that prides itself on its commitment to 'inspire and nurture the human spirit'. The furore and protests against Starbucks resulted in it apologising for the incident, reaching financial settlement with Rashon Nelson and Donte Robinson, and shutting down all of its 8,000 branches to give its employees racial bias training.

Would Holly Hylton have called the police on White customers who didn't buy something while waiting for friends or White people who she claimed didn't speak good English? No, of course not. There was something inherently dangerous to her about the Black identity of Rashon Nelson and Donte Robinson, which draws from a long history of criminalising and dehumanising Black men. She was simply offended by their presence. Such presence is in the context of what Black identity is to her and how dangerous it is if it does not conform. This triggered her weaponisation of Whiteness not because they broke the law or broke some non-existent Starbucks policy, where you are not allowed to wait for a friend before buying a Starbucks product, but because they are Black. There was also a false notion of fault ascribed to these men by the presence of the police. People were ready to believe Black people must have done something wrong, however little, to justify the presence of the police. This sort of thinking is biased and trivialises the pervasive effects of White supremacy.

According to both men, they were never asked to leave, they didn't refuse to buy something, but had explained they were waiting for a friend before doing so and waiting in Starbucks is not unusual for most patrons of its stores. This was subsequently proven following their arrest. These critical facts were missing from media headlines, which led many to believe it was them who had refused to leave and the call to the police was therefore warranted. This is without consideration of why, presumably, 'going to the bathroom' or 'waiting for a friend' would be grounds for the manager to tell them to leave, which never happened. There is no doubt in my mind that Holly Hylton knew her report to the police was false and that by calling the police she could potentially unjustly deny them their liberty or, at worst, cost them their lives. What she did was racist.

AMY COOPER

In May 2020, Amy Cooper went viral for calling the police on an African American man, **Christian Cooper** (no relation), who had asked her to put a leash on her dog in accordance with the rules of the wooded area of New York's Central Park called the Ramble. In response to this, Amy Cooper proceeded to intimidate him by firstly threatening to call the police, and then calling the police to say 'there's a man, African American, he has a bicycle helmet. He is recording me and threatening me and my dog.' It was not just that she called the police, but it was her intent in doing so, knowing the threat of the police to a Black life. She knew her power as a White woman would trigger the use of force against this Black man. Her act was heinous, callous and without a doubt wicked. She drew on a long, violent and painful history of dehumanising Black people. Be in no doubt that Christian Cooper was potentially a George Floyd. He was potentially an Emmett Till, the fourteen-year-old boy who was lynched in 1955 for 'offending' a White woman, Carolyn Bryant. What was his offence? He was accused of flirting with her. Carolyn Bryant confessed decades later that she had lied about it. Just as the killing of George Floyd led to global #BlackLivesMatter protests in

2020, the killing of fourteen-year-old Emmett Till in 1955 was one of the catalysts of the Civil Rights movement.

There is no doubt that what was so offensive in the Jim Crow-era was that fourteen-year-old Emmett had crossed some invisible barrier of conduct acceptable between an African American male and a White woman. Notwithstanding that he was a child, he was beaten, brutalised and shot in the head for having the audacity to 'flirt' with a White woman. Amy Cooper's intimidation of Christian Cooper was borne out of that same inherent sense of 'how dare this Black not know his place' that Carolyn Bryant manifested against Emmet Till. Both women weaponised their Whiteness against these African American males for offending them, NOT for breaking the law. Not only did Amy Cooper call the police, if you watch the video you can hear the way she manipulates the tone of her voice to sound like she's frightened, threatened and in deep fear of her life. This truly captured the imagination of many White people, allowing them to finally see behaviour such as this as racist. No Black person I know was shocked by her behaviour or needed to see a video to imagine it even if they were being told the details directly by Christian Cooper. But because denial of racism and obliviousness to its insidious manifestation in the lives of Black people is quite commonplace with many White people, they were in shock. Some White people turned from doubting Thomases to believers. It took a video to make them see and understand what we have been telling them for centuries.

Interestingly enough, it is in the lack of awareness that there is a direct correlation between racist Amy Cooper of New York's Central Park and the same Amy Cooper who worked as Head of Insurance Investments at Franklin Templeton. Racism is no respecter of location. Just as she demonstrated racist behaviour to a perfect stranger in Central Park because she was offended, imagine for one second what she must be like with Black subordinates or direct reports who offend her at work. She was fired by Franklin Templeton within 48 hours of the video going viral. In an interview with CNN, in which she apologised, Amy Cooper reiterated the age-old defence of racists: 'I'm not a racist. I did not mean to harm that man in any way'. She goes on to say: 'I was just scared'. This is nonsense. Just like Holly Hylton, Amy Cooper drew from a long history of criminalising and dehumanising Black men. She was simply offended by his audacity to ask her to follow the rules and put a leash on her dog. This triggered her to weaponise her Whiteness, not because Christian Cooper broke the law or because he was wrong that she had broken the Ramble rule of keeping dogs on a leash, but because she was offended.

Without a doubt, what Amy Cooper did was intentionally and objectively racist. She feigned fear for her life using trigger words that would get the police running to the rescue of a White woman. Aside from referring to him as African American in quite a frightened tone, she says these words sounding increasingly distressed: 'I'm being threatened by a man in the Ramble. Please send the cops immediately!' It is evident she meant Christian Cooper harm and wanted to see harm done to him. It was probably not until the furore from her actions – the direct consequences of losing her job, surrendering her dog to the dog shelter she got him from and the immense public backlash from both sides of the pond – that Amy Cooper understood that the world views her actions as racist. Living as a Black person has literally become a mastermind exercise to breathe. Try to imagine for a second how incredibly insane it must be that Black people cannot go about their everyday routine activities without having to answer to White people (not all White people, but some) who treat them suspiciously and make demands on them like it is their God-given right. *We can't breathe.*

For instance, in 2018, CNN reported over twenty incidents of daily activities for which African Americans were reported to the police by some White Americans. These included but were not limited to 'golfing too slowly; barbecuing at a park; working out at a gym; campaigning door to door; moving into an apartment; mowing the wrong lawn; shopping for prom clothes; napping in a university common room; asking for directions; not waving while leaving an Airbnb; redeeming a coupon; selling bottled water on a sidewalk; eating lunch on a college campus; riding in a car with a white grandmother; babysitting two white children; wearing a backpack that brushed against a woman; working as a home inspector; working as a firefighter; helping a homeless man; delivering newspapers; swimming in a pool; shopping while pregnant; driving with leaves on a car; and trying to cash a pay check'.[*]

Social media now plays a significant role in sharing these incidents to a much wider audience and faster than traditional media, which does a poor job in reporting these incidents and, when reported, it is usually biased against the Black person. If CNN could report over twenty of such incidents with little effort, there is no doubt there are many more not caught on camera or not reported. What is evident is that there are some White people who are desperate to deputise as police and use that authority to ostensibly confront and victimise Black people to the point of intimidating and threatening them with violence. This also goes to show that the police play a significant role as the existential affirmation of weaponising Whiteness and as the authority to execute the pressure of the White Knee on Black Necks.

---

[*] Brandon Griggs, 'Here are all the routine activities for which police were called on African Americans this year', CNN, 28 December 2018, https://edition.cnn.com/2018/12/20/us/living-while-black-police-calls-trnd/index.html.

In Britain, many in the Black community experience being stopped and searched by the police for doing normal daily activities. Black people are more than four times as likely to be stopped and searched as White people without any finding of wrongdoing. This was revealed in an analysis commissioned by the *Guardian*, which further showed that stop and searches on Black British were less likely to detect crime than those conducted on White people.[*] The analysis went on to show that, in 2018, 43% of 151,103 people stopped and searched in London by the police were Black and 35.5% were White. Black people only made up 15.6% of London's population, while White people made up 59.8%. Once again, it goes to show that Black skin is the probable *cause* for the disproportionate discriminatory treatment, with the resulting *effect* of making Black people fit the supposed crime or non-criminal offence of going about their daily mundane business.

CONCLUDING THOUGHTS . . .

The mantra 'Britain is the least racist country in the world' is chanted on repeat to comfort White British who are either complacent on the issue of race, racism and race inclusion or to comfort racists who want to deny the full extent of their complicity in benefiting from and reproducing racism. 'Least racist' is cold comfort and by no means a solution for Black people and Ethnic Minorities whose experiences can attest to the fact that there is no such thing as 'least racist'. Britain is indeed institutionally racist and so is the United

---

[*] Vikram Dodd, 'Met police "disproportionately" use stop and search powers on black people', *Guardian*, 26 January 2019, https://www.theguardian.com/law/2019/jan/26/met-police-disproportionately-use-stop-and-search-powers-on-black-people.

States of America. Outcomes for Black people reflect the opposite of 'least racist' to be true. Emergent Blacks, Asians and Ethnic Minorities still struggle in present-day America and Britain against racism and prejudice. The racial disparities are in the outcomes. That is where the 'ability to breathe' becomes completely constricted. The journey does not end there, because for many Black people we have to go through it again to try to reach a different outcome against the odds. This could be education, employment, better housing, etc.; we keep working hard, striving for a different outcome. Where one door is shut in our faces as a result of racism, a lifetime of experience teaches us to keep pushing or try a new path. It is no longer just a breathing exercise but training ourselves to exhale even when there appears to be no reason to.

Health disparities

The coronavirus pandemic effectively magnified longstanding structural inequalities that are exemplified by the high rate of Covid deaths among Black, Asian and Ethnic Minorities. There is direct causation between the systemic intersecting inequalities fueled by institutional racism and the rising Covid death toll on these groups. To put it simply, the socio-economic disadvantages imposed on them exacerbates their exposure to Covid-19. This is the discriminatory impact of the virus and why Black, Asian and Ethnic Minorities were disproportionately affected by it in Britain and America. There is no doubt that there is a direct link between health and socio-economic inequalities.

In Britain and America, the death toll of Covid-19 has been particularly devastating for Black people. A study by the UK Intensive Care National Audit & Research Centre showed an ethnic breakdown of the impact of the virus in Britain, which revealed

Covid-19 disproportionately impacts Black, Asian and Ethnic Minorities in comparison to White people. In America, according to APM Research, 'African Americans have died at a rate of 50.3 per 100,000 people, compared with 20.7 for whites, 22.9 for Latinos and 22.7 for Asian Americans'.[*] Interesting to note that rather than focus on addressing the root causes of systemic structural inequalities, some schools of thought chose to blame culture and physiological reasons as the cause of the high rate of Covid deaths from the Black, Asian and Ethnic Minority communities. Everything from our food, way of life to biological reasons are to blame for Covid-19 death rates, was their position. This is, of course, not true and deliberately misleading, so as not to address how the coronavirus pandemic shines a light on the disparities and the deadly legacy of structural inequality. There seems to be a reluctance to fix the problems that structural inequalities cause in exacerbating Covid-19, even though Public Health England found that racism and discrimination are root causes of inequality and that increases exposure to Covid-19.[†] *We can't breathe.*

Work disparities

In comparison to their White work colleagues, Black people face more obstacles to securing employment and/or getting promoted. Unemployment rates continue to reflect fewer job opportunitites, less pay, unequal outcomes and fewer opportunities. Without a doubt,

---

[*] Ed Pilkington, 'Black Americans dying of Covid-19 at three times the rate of white people', *Guardian*, 20 May 2020, https://www.theguardian.com/world/2020/may/20/black-americans-death-rate-covid-19-coronavirus.

[†] 'Coronavirus: Racism "could play a part in BAME Covid deaths"', BBC, 13 June 2020, https://www.bbc.co.uk/news/health-53035054?ocid=wsnews.chat-apps.in-app-msg.whatsapp.trial.link1_.auin.

the barriers faced are systemic and rooted in institutional racism that results in poorer-quality jobs and benefits, evident discrimination in pay disparitites between Black and White counterparts and with zero-hours contracts being more accessible than stable well-paying jobs. Occupational steering, pay inequality and outright discrimination are only a few of the obstacles Black people deal with. According to the UK Government official unemployment figures, '4% of White people were unemployed in 2018, compared with 7% of people from all other ethnic groups combined. Black people had the highest unemployment rate out of all the ethnic groups (9%).'* Furthermore, it revealed that, across the UK, unemployment rates were lower for White people than for all other ethnic groups combined. In America, the Economic Policy Institute shared its findings about the persistent racial disparities Black workers experience in employment outcomes compared to their White counterparts.[†] These findings also include data that concluded that Black workers are less likely than White workers to be employed in a job that is consistent with their level of education, and that Black workers are twice as likely to be unemployed as White workers at almost every education level. *We can't breathe.*

Crime

The fact that Black communities experience increasing levels of knife crime in Britain and gun crime in America is not a reason to deny Black people good policing and protection. The British and American

---

* UK Govt Ethnicity and figures, https://www.ethnicity-facts-figures.service.gov.uk/work-pay-and-benefits/unemployment-and-economic-inactivity/unemployment/latest#main-facts-and-figures.

† Jhacova Williams and Valerie Wilson, 'Black workers endure persistent racial disparities in employment outcomes', Economic Policy Institute, 27 August 2019, https://www.epi.org/publication/labor-day-2019-racial-disparities-in-employment/.

police forces are there to serve and protect Black communities too. It does not justify police brutality or the discriminatory treatment in the outcomes of investigating and prosecuting crimes against Black people. Crimes committed by or against a Black person cannot constantly be blamed on the one-size-fits-all racist trope about single mothers and absent fathers. It is evidence of a failed State when a demographic of the State is inadequately protected from crime, including police brutality, and disproportionately incarcerated and sentenced for crimes committed compared to its White counterparts.

The use of the term 'Black on Black' crime as a racial pathology of Black people is racist and without substance. After all, there are 'White on White' crimes that are statistically worse, but this does not create a pathology of violence for White people. Furthermore, the false equivalence of 'Black on Black' crime to police brutality against Black people or entrenched systemic institutional racism endured by Black people is prejudiced. Detractors imply that Black communities are not doing enough to address 'Black on Black' crime and question why there is more outrage at police brutality than about deaths from 'Black on Black' crimes. This is just more disingenuity and gaslighting to discredit the fight against police brutality. 'Black on Black' crime, just like 'White on White' crime, has nothing to do with race but everything to do with motive, opportunity, proximity and poverty. Murder and crime are not a Black pathology. Racism is not the cause of 'Black on Black' crime and it is a double standard that 'Black on Black' crime is pushed as racial pathology rather than 'White on White', which is referred to as simply a crime. It is a deliberate tactic to pathologise the Black identity as violent and criminal so we can be blamed for racially motivated acts against us as well as crimes against each other.

We can't breathe.

4

WHO'S PLAYING THE RACE CARD?

'For those of us called White, Whiteness simply is. Whiteness becomes, for us, the unspoken, uninterrogated norm, taken for granted, much as water can be taken for granted by a fish.'*

American activist, Tim Wise

If there was ever a 'race card' to play, then the White race card is the biggest race card played in the modern history of the human race. Not only are White people uniquely placed to play with a full deck every single day, it applies to every single one of them whether they consciously or sub-consciously benefit from and/or reproduce this race card. Without a shadow of a doubt, the White race card is the default position of British and American societies, and is normalised as White privilege. As a result, it legitimises and reinforces White supremacy. But do you find the idiomatic phrase 'playing the race card' used by Black people and Ethnic Minorities against White people? No. In fact, it is the beneficiaries of the biggest race card ever played who coined 'playing the race card' as a strategy and tool to silence Black people when we call out racism and try to explain our

---

* Tim Wise, *White Like Me: Reflections on Race from a Privileged Son*, Soft Skull Press, 2004.

lived experiences of it. The phrase is not used by all White people, only some. It is used by racists, enablers of White supremacy and deniers of our lived experience of racism. Its use is deeply racially prejudiced. It is not lost on me that there are self-serving Black people and Ethnic Minorities who use this phrase to destabilise anti-racism efforts and discredit lived experiences of racism, thereby legitimising the racist attacks against Black people. These are racial gatekeepers and I will discuss their influence in the dehumanisation of the Black identity later in this chapter.

The use of 'playing the race card' is the transference of a false equivalence of privilege to Black people that has no substance or bearing in the real world. I think, in the minds of racists and deniers of racism, metaphorically referring to anti-racism as 'playing the race card' is an attempt to delegitimise the consequences that come with the public condemnation of racist behaviour, such as job loss, loss of financial backing/sponsorship, critical reputational damage, etc. This is colloquially referred to as 'cancel culture', in which those who have behaved in a racist manner to Black people and Ethnic Minorities play the victim as though they should not suffer any consequences or not be held accountable. The attempt to shame and undermine Black people into silence is the reason for shutting down our experiences with 'they are playing the race card'. This so-called 'playing the race card' affords us zero advantages. This is about Black lives and speaking out about our hurt, frustration and dehumanising experiences of racism, it is our outlet to breathe. It is not a race card to play neither is it a race to win, because by confronting abusers, accusers and racists head on we are saying to enforcers and enablers of White supremacy that we will no longer play or live by their rules. These are rules requiring us to internalise lived experiences of racism, ignore the erosion of our dignity and relegation to second-class citizens, like the concocted image of the White man's happy Black slave, who danced to the tune of the slave master with a watermelon smile. In the words of Zora Neale Hurston, 'If you are silent about your pain, they'll kill you and say you enjoyed it.'*

The agenda for accusing Black people of playing the race card is to whitewash structural racism, as we have seen in Chapter One, and trivialise real experiences of racial discrimination. This strategy of accusatory attack against Black people, rather than using it as an opportunity to unlearn racist behaviour, is not new. In fact, many Black people hurting from discrimination choose not to say anything, or struggle to voice their suffering, out of fear of being accused of 'playing the race card'. It takes a lot of courage and boldness for a Black person to reclaim their right to speak up, not knowing if they will be believed or if it will cost them their job, reputation or dignity, as has been the open practice for centuries. The stigmatisation of this accusation is perceived wrongly by some to outweigh the victimisation of racism they are suffering. This is unacceptable. Victims of racial discrimination should not be bullied into fear of speaking out. The fear of 'playing the race card' is how victims of oppression silenced from speaking out can lead to nationwide inaction in confronting racism. This inevitably leads to the misappropriation of the Black identity. This was exemplified in football when ex-BBC Soccer pundit and former midfielder, Derby County footballer Craig Ramage racially stereotyped young Black footballers in February 2020. His comments were that 'young, black lads' at Championship side Derby County 'need pulling down a peg or two' because of their body language, stance, wealth etc. Ramage exemplified how racial stereotyping of Black people and misappropriation of the Black identity is normalised in so many professional sectors:

---

* Zora Neale Hurston, Author of *Their Eyes Were Watching God*.

'When I look over and look at certain players, their body language, their stance, the way they act, you just feel, hold on a minute, he needs pulling down a peg or two. So I'd probably say that about all the young black lads [. . .].'*

The fact that he felt so comfortable saying this tells me he says it often, that it's probably a common view, held by him, others in his circle and within the football profession. He definitely felt comfortable enough to say it on a publicly broadcast podcast without fear of consequences. Racism in British football isn't new, but Ramage's choice of words is everyday language that could easily be that of a White line manager in a corporate setting, a White bank manager to a Black entrepreneur or White school teacher to Black kids or White police to Black youth, etc. 'Pulling down a peg or two' is just another way of saying the racial stereotype 'uppity', to, in his words, put these young Black footballers in their place. It smacks of intolerance and jealousy, as though they are yet to earn their stripes. Footballer Max Lowe, twenty-two years old at the time, called Ramage out on behalf of Black footballers at Derby County. He shared the transcript of Ramage's words on Instagram and explained:

'Racial ignorance, stereotyping and intolerance negatively affects the image of impressionable young footballers and creates an unnecessary divide in society. I am also disappointed that a public service broadcaster did not step in to ask the analyst to explain his reasoning, or to distance themselves from these archaic thoughts.'†

---

* BBC Sportscene podcast, 15 February 2020.
† BBC Sports, 'Derby County's Max Lowe criticises pundit's "racial ignorance" in BBC broadcast', https://www.bbc.co.uk/sport/football/51526053.

Following Max Lowe's condemnation of Ramage and the public backlash, BBC Radio Derby fired Craig Ramage and both it and Derby County FC fully condemned and distanced themselves from him.

When Edward Enninful was racially profiled in July 2020 at his place of work, where he is editor of British *Vogue*, it caused some waves of surprise and indignation that he was told to use the loading bay to gain entrance and not the front entrance. Being racially profiled is not uncommon for Black people and I don't know any Black person who is ever surprised when such experiences are shared. There are a range of racial stereotypes, bias and microaggressions we face that have no bearing on who we are or what we represent. The racial bias that Black people are for menial work, don't belong and should go through the back door is part of the legacy of slavery and colonialism in Britain and America. It is racism and anti-Black. This is *not* 'playing the race card'.

There is also a mistaken belief that racial bias and stereotype don't happen to high-profile and successful Black people, when nothing could be further from the truth. Even billionaire Oprah Winfrey, one of the world's richest women and most famous faces, was denied a handbag she was considering buying in a Swiss store because the shop assistant said it was 'too expensive'.* Racism does not respect our achievements and accomplishments. Though Oprah's money was the right colour, her skin colour was a barrier to that shop assistant. Although Enninful had every right to walk through the front door, his skin colour was a barrier to that security guard, who told him to go through the loading bay to gain entrance. This is racism and anti-Black. This is *not* 'playing the race card'.

---

* Nick Thompson and Diana Magnay, 'Oprah Winfrey racism row over Switzerland shop incident', CNN, 11 August 2013, https://edition.cnn.com/2013/08/09/world/oprah-winfrey-racism-switzerland/index.html.

I was racially profiled as a cleaner when I went to do a political commentary at RT UK News in 2019. I informed the security guard at Millbank Centre that I was there to do a TV interview and the name of the media company. He took my ID to write a pass and then asked me if I was a cleaner. I was genuinely baffled, but my sixth sense knew what was coming. I asked him why he would ask if I was a cleaner. His immediate response was 'because we send cleaners to the back'. I can honestly say that at this point I was tired. Tired that we have to go through this time and time again because of people's ignorance and racial bias. I asked him why he would ask me if I was a cleaner *after* I had informed him I was there to do a TV interview with RT UK News. He could not answer. I challenged him on what it was about me that says 'cleaner'. He could not answer. I gave him a piece of my mind. I reported him to the manager of the building, who apologised profusely for his behaviour and to RT UK News, which offered their unreserved apology. The security guard did not apologise to me. By the time I had done my TV interview, he had left for the day.

What is interesting are those who cast doubt on our experiences and even seek to trivialise it by false comparison. When I shared my experience on social media, I was not surprised to see comments in my mentions questioning what I looked like. It was shameful for anyone to think there are any grounds that could excuse the security guard's behaviour. There are clearly people out there who will always call what is objectively racist behaviour anything but racist. I did share a tweet of what I looked like doing the TV interview, but it left a sour taste that my experience would be discounted and not believed as a racial incident. While this does not surprise me, it leaves me with the irrefutable truth that racial profiling and denial of racist behaviour are not signs of a progressive society. We still have a long way to go.

ANTI-RACISM IS NOT ANTI-WHITE

'Let us be dissatisfied until integration is not seen as a problem but as an opportunity to participate in the beauty of diversity. Let us be dissatisfied until men and women, however black they may be, will be judged on the basis of the content of their character, not on the basis of the color of their skin. Let us be dissatisfied.'*

Martin Luther King Jr

I am dissatisfied. I am angry and I will not be silenced. Neither will I be told how to express my dissatisfaction or tone my voice to make White people comfortable with the ugliness of the racism that some of them perpetuate and regarding which others are not doing nearly enough to stop. I am no longer convinced they just don't know. I am fully convinced that, unless a White person was born yesterday, any ignorance of institutional racism is perverse and wilful. Neither are others doing nearly enough to educate themselves. Instead, those who choose to be are complacent and complicit in feeding anti-racist activists to White supremacists. Seeing the damage and threats posed to our lives as none of their business and justly deserved. While others take the high road of leaving the responsibility to Black people to do the learning and unlearning for them. Forget it – I'm done with that.

To anti-racist activists like me, accusations of 'playing the race card', 'anti-White', 'race-baiter', 'racist' and 'virtue signaller' have become the normal surge of abuse thrown at us to combat our anti-racism efforts. It is clear these racists and deniers of racism

* Martin Luther King Jr, 'Where Do We Go From Here?', address delivered at the Eleventh Annual SCLC Convention, 16 August 1967.

cannot handle the truth we speak and the fragility of their White ego is at breaking point. White people rationalise their racist history with Black people as justifiable, resulting in the stigma of the Black identity, the focus of which became the subject of systemic inequality and institutional racism. To attack activists as anti-White or accuse us of racism for speaking out against the pervasive systemic inequality and insidious nature of institutional racism that currently exists is the White people's failed attempt at false equivalence. This is the direct result of the legacy of British and American history of slavery. Be in no doubt that this is a strategy to ferociously deny Black people justice and to deny us a voice by any means necessary, even if it demonstrates their ignorance, White privilege, self-entitlement, and at the cost of the life and liberty of Black people. James Baldwin aptly describes this condition of White society when he says: 'It is certain, in any case, that ignorance, allied with power, is the most ferocious enemy justice can have.'*

These racists, and deniers of Black people's lived experience of racism, are more outraged by the so-called 'playing the race card' than by racist behaviour which negatively impacts Black lives. It is reprehensible that *we* not only have to deal with institutional racism, and defend ourselves from racism, but we are also expected to explain that racism to the very people who perpetuate the racism, and then bear the brunt of the denials of those perpetrators that our lived experience of racism does not exist. We are done with that.

Being anti-racist does not mean anti-White. Those triggered by the boldness of anti-racists are looking to discredit the anti-racism efforts and displace responsibility for institutional racism on to those who do not benefit from or reproduce it. Additionally, the anti-racist equals anti-White mantra makes no sense because not all White people

---

* James Baldwin, *No Name in the Street*, Dial Press, 1972.

are racists and anti-racism is not about hating White people. White supremacy is founded on the premise of racial superiority, the justification for which is to dehumanise those considered as an 'inferior race' for the sole benefit of the superior White race. There is nothing superior about the White race. There never was and never will be.

The first time I recall being called a 'race-baiter' live on air was by Piers Morgan during a heated debate about Harry and Meghan in January 2020 on ITV's *Good Morning Britain*. Morgan did not believe nor agree with my views on how racism had contributed to the biased coverage of Meghan, Duchess of Sussex, by the British media. It was only after this debate, in which we both didn't give an inch, that I noticed how emboldened trolls and the like became with using the term 'race-baiter' in their online abuse against me. Getting abuse online is nothing new to me, but the use of 'race-baiter' as well as 'racist' escalated significantly, particularly because my position was centred on the wider issue of the UK as an institutionally racist country. Some White people don't recognise what they do not experience and are unwilling to unlearn their wilful ignorance and obliviousness to the state of institutional racism. Prominent British voices in the anti-racist efforts, such as Afua Hirsch, Ayesha Hazarika, Dr Kehinde Andrews, David Olusoga and many more, also faced the same barrage of accusations and online abuse. Social media became a circus of dissenting and concurring views, on the one hand demanding examples of racism against Meghan and on the other providing the examples, going back and forth. When asked for examples, I refused to play their mindless game against us, especially when a plethora of evidence was already available to them. Neither was I going to respond to some White people's demand that I treat them like they are judge and jury over what racism is to Black people and Ethnic Minorities. Who the heck died and made them god? Social media, as usual, was awash with differing views like these tweets:

Loustar @weatherston49 Jun 9 2020

> Replying to @GMB and @SholaMos1
> This woman is so unbelievably racist and GMT's is
> encouraging her ludicrous ideas. Everyone is equal and
> we should not be trying to convince young black people
> that they are oppressed and that it's ok the destroy other
> people's property!

Ezmaralda @Miniature_Miss Jan 16 2020

> Replying to @darylking and @SholaMos1
> Behave! This is utterly disgusting. Doesn't matter how
> black, female or many degrees this person has, shola mos
> is nothing more than a race baiter.

Kate Morrison @katemorrison Jan 13 2020

> Replying to @The_JamesJordan
> She said absolutely nothing that was racist. She explained
> calmly and clearly how a racist system excuses, denies or
> glosses over racist comments / actions such as the media's
> coverage of Meghan Markle. You're just proving her point
> by trying to turn the argument against her.

MICROAGGRESSIONS

The accusatory mindset of 'playing the race card' also reveals itself through racial microaggressions. One of the hidden agendas of the 'playing the race card' narrative is to whitewash racial micro-aggressions underpinning its surface. These are verbal and non-verbal indignities, insults and demeaning messages sent to Black people and Ethnic Minorities by White people, particularly those who appear well intentioned. The term microaggression was first coined by psychiatrist Chester M. Pierce, MD, in the 1970s, but its application in discourse today as racial microaggression can be credited to Derald Wing Sue, a professor of counselling psychology at Columbia University.

The insidious nature of racism expresses itself in overt and covert ways using the machinations of microaggression, causing untold debilitating impacts on the quality of life and choice of Black people. These microaggressions more often than not impede Black people from accessing opportunities and resources. Microaggressions are not only demonstrated by 'bad people' with bad intentions, or only by people who consciously think or act overtly that the White race is superior, but are demonstrated by White work colleagues, school teachers, bus drivers, bar tenders, etc., not just the people you would expect to use the 'nigger' word, say, like those with Nazi signs tattooed on them or those who carry burning crosses. White people we get on with and know as good people are also capable of demonstrating these microaggressions, thereby benefiting from and reproducing the system of White supremacy. These racial aggressions come from well-intentioned White people who consider themselves good, decent human beings with not a racist bone in their body. If you're Black, Asian or Ethnic Minority and tired of racial microaggressions, or do not realise as a White person that you are micro-aggressive, then it is time to confront and challenge.

Every fibre of my being is ready to confront and challenge the micro-aggressive behaviours of racism. If anyone is going to be silenced, it won't be me. Uncomfortable conversations about racial microaggressions are a good starting point. To White people I say, this is not the time to fold your hands doing nothing but the time to confront your bias. This is the way we begin the much-needed work to end institutional racism and the varying forms of racial stereotypes, conscious and sub-conscious bias, and racial prejudice inflicted on Black people and Ethnic Minorities because of their race. It is important to understand the impact of these racial micro-aggressions from the perspective of the people being victimised. Well-intentioned White people must take responsibility for deter-mining the whys and wherefores of their subconscious prejudice and biased language or behaviour. If they do not, they will keep demonstrating racial microaggressions towards Black people and Ethnic Minorities.

Writing this chapter is my contribution to educating micro-aggressors. Beyond this I am reserving my energy to deal with the microaggressions that come the way of those victimised by it. I do think we must challenge these behaviours head on when confronted with them. This educates micro-aggressors. I encourage every Black person to tackle these microaggressions as they present themselves, be it in the board room, at a social engagement, on the high street, in school, or even Downing Street and the White House. I appreciate we all have to pick our battles, but once it is picked, be without fear in providing swift correction to the individual. Remember micro-aggressions don't come with notice, so be prepared.

Here are some excellent examples of daily racial micro-aggressions and what you could say:

1. *'I'm not a racist. I have mixed-race children, my partner is Black or I have Black friends.'*

This is the micro-aggressor's attempt to insinuate they have a free licence to call the oppression and expression of Black peo-ple's experience of racism as anything other than racist because they know what it is to be Black by their close association with the Black people in their lives. It is nonsense, totally ignoring how interpersonal relationships are shaped and not evidence of non-racist behaviour to those outside your close circle.

What to say: inform the micro-aggressor that proximity to Black people does not immunise them from saying or doing something racist. Explain how this is a defence used by every racist and that it proves, if anything, that personal relationships with Black people does not substitute for their benefiting from or reinforcing White supremacy. It is a terrible excuse for racism.

2. *'I believe the most qualified person should get the job.'*

This statement is the racist justification for meritocracy. It implies that good jobs are being taken away from the most qualified and sacrificed for a marginalised group in the name of diversity. It suggests those in this marginalised group are not good enough and are being given an unfair advantage over White people because they are Black. It is a racially micro-aggressive insult with racist undertones.

What to say: inform the micro-aggressor this is racist because it implies that Black people and Ethnic Minorities would not have the requisite qualifications for the job and it is a handout at the expense of qualified White people. It suggests Black people and Ethnic Minorities are lazy and should work harder. It also implies that Black people who secure those jobs got them only through affirmative action or a quota system and not because they earned and deserved it.

3. *'Where are you <u>really</u> from?'*

This statement immediately puts the recipient on notice that they are perceived not to belong and are foreigners. There is nothing innocuous about this question, especially because the use of the word 'really' suggests it has been asked at least once by the same person but they are not satisfied by the initial response given. The question ultimately expands to 'where are your parents from' or 'where's your accent from', in order to pin you down to a box that fits their perception of where people that look or sound like you come from.

What to say: inform the micro-aggressor that their question is inappropriate because it suggests the recipient of the question is not who they say they are. Explain it gives the impression the recipient is not truly British or American or comes from somewhere else and does not belong. It is rude and racist. Flip the question and make the micro-aggressor uncomfortable. Challenge them by asking what about the initial answer makes them doubt where you say you are from. Alternatively, ask them where they are really from and challenge them that, if they think being White suffices for an explanation of being British or American, they clearly don't know their history.

Sometimes, racial microaggressions tend to come from what appears to be a place of curiosity or harmless small talk, but the truth underlying this façade is a suspicion or fear (whether rational or irrational) that there is something different about the Black person. It is exhausting having to appear okay with it, especially when these microaggressions take place all the time and the micro-aggressors can't take a hint. It is equally exhausting that, when those experiencing racial microaggressions confront their abusers, they are accused of being 'woke'.

THE WEAPONISATION OF 'WOKE'

Being 'woke' has become a politicised term weaponised to further the 'playing the race card' agenda of racists and deniers of lived experiences of racism. For ease of reference, I will refer to those weaponising 'woke' as the anti-woke. I do not think being 'woke' is to be on the left or right wing of public thought or the political spectrum, but it seems the right wing of politics now claim 'woke' as a tool of the Left to hijack social justice. As someone who is politically homeless, I know this to be untrue. The point I am addressing here is that those who are 'woke' to social injustice are attacked by those who see that awakening as an attack on their freedom to disagree social injustice exists, hence they are the anti-woke. 'Woke' is a colloquial term.

'Woke' was first coined by African Americans as a call to be vigilant about social and racial justice, but unfortunately wokeness has evolved into being weaponised to silence actions for that very same justice. Accusations of wokeness add tensions to the race and discrimination debate rather than being used as a common stance of all sides regarding vigilance for social and racial justice. Dissenters of justice now use 'woke' as an insult to accuse anti-racists of silencing free speech in order to manipulate arguments on racial tensions in their favour. Nothing could be further from the truth, but just like 'playing the race card', 'woke' is weaponised to delegitimise Black people's lived experiences of racism. Under the false guise of protecting free speech, 'woke' is being rebranded as 'political correctness gone wrong' and an attempt to 'cancel' those who speak opposing views on racism and discrimination. It is shocking that something as justifiable as liberty and freedom for the marginalised, social justice and equality, and human rights for all is objectionable to some. In any decent society, surely the debate should never be on the *what* but on the *how*? Not *if* we should, but that we must end racism and discrimination. It is madness that history is literally repeating itself at a time when it should serve to remind us how far wrong we can go if we don't unite. Injustice and inequality come in different shapes, but particularly for Black people, these injustices and inequalities intersect and are systemic, so it is critical that, as a society, we are socially and politically 'woke' to it and equally adamant to bring an end to it.

The anti-woke who deny social injustice are afraid of being mischaracterised or misinterpreted. However, that fear is not reserved for the anti-woke alone. It works both ways and happens to those who are 'woke' to social justice too. The fear of threats and abuse both offline and online is a constant experience for the woke, stoked by the anti-woke. The anti-woke efforts to delegitimise the anti-racism efforts by creating toxic environments for debate and discourse is the constant experience for the woke. The anti-woke want the world to believe they are the victims here and that their right to freedom of speech is being held hostage on issues of race and discrimination. Nothing could be further from the truth. The real victims here are Black lives and it is their quality of life and choice being held hostage by those who are desperate to keep the status quo. The status quo for the anti-woke way of life is predicated on the denial of an equal value of life and liberty for Black people. More so, is how much the anti-woke seemingly despise taking responsibility for their own actions, claiming 'cancel culture' is leftist and punishment for speaking their minds, which is their right. It begs the question, why are the anti-woke so fearful of the so-called 'cancel culture'? Journalist Owen

Jones comes to mind when I think of the anti-woke assertions of cancel culture. He aptly captures how ineffective the cancel culture is if it is:

'being used to describe everything from people disapproving of paedophiles to celebrities being criticised on social media. It's become a means to protect the powerful and wealthy from being scrutinised for things they say or do.'*

There is no such thing as 'cancel culture'. Certainly not the 'leftist-manipulating-freedom-of-speech-denying' apocalypse the anti-woke would have the world believe. According to columnist Andrew Doyle, 'those who self-identify as woke would sooner intimidate their detractors into silence through what has become known as "cancel culture".'† I disagree. It is called having a difference of opinion, debate, discourse and so on and so forth, but comes with consequences that the public control. It seems the anti-woke have double standards of epic proportions – it is 'detractors' when they give their opinion, but 'intimidation' when the woke give theirs. It's brain-exhausting!

I believe in holding those responsible accountable for their actions, which can take various forms depending on the totality of the circumstances. In many situations in life, there are loads of grey shades to navigate and very little black and white, and some things are not just right or wrong. People make mistakes, learn from those mistakes or are misunderstood and mis-characterised.

---

* Owen Jones, Sky News interview on Cancel Culture, 11 July 2020, https://twitter.com/OwenJones84/status/1281957010880307201?s=20.
† Andrew Doyle, 'Why I'm Anti-Woke', *Spiked*, 5 February 2020, https://www.spiked-online.com/2020/02/05/why-im-anti-woke/.

Society today does itself no favours in not recognising the complex nature of humanity or layers of nuances in discourse or debates. I can get into a passionate and heated debate with an opposing view and shake hands at the end. It is not personal and doesn't have to be unless the other person makes it so. I cannot imagine the legal or medical profession falling apart because of difference of opinions. Woke or anti-woke, freedom of speech comes with consequences and responsibility. It seems what the anti-woke stress about is social media denouncing a person or product that no longer has merit in their view. But surely if freedom of speech is the cornerstone of the anti-woke, they should respect that other people have freedom of speech too? By no longer following someone, watching their movies or buying their product, we see freedom of speech in motion. That is the right of people to speak their mind. This has been happening long before social media existed. Say what you want, but there'll be consequences.

Sounds to me as if the anti-woke want to share difference of opinions, including polarising views that can negatively impact the anti-racism efforts, without accountability for the impact of their words and actions. Their denial of social injustice is purely to preserve the status quo of White supremacy, which is predicated on denying an equal value of life and liberty to Black people. This includes racial gatekeepers whose proximity to the tentacles of White supremacy is purely for self-preservation.

RACIAL GATEKEEPERS

I am going to cut to the chase. The dehumanisation, commoditisation, misrepresentation and marginalisation of the Black identity is not complete without the self-serving token Black or Ethnic

Minority who is ready to sell out their race for self-preservation. These are progress blockers whose sole aim is to protect and preserve White privilege and White supremacy because they benefit from it by proximity. These racial gatekeepers use their voice, power and/or influence to discredit and undermine the anti-racism efforts. This is not about a difference of opinion but the deliberate legitimisation of the racist and prejudiced views, and the support of such actions and policies, which will put Black people at a significant disadvantage, or the intent of upholding the status quo of denying an equal value of life and liberty of Black people. The legitimacy they give does not speak to the veracity of the issue in question but to embolden racists and White supremacists, so they think that their acts, words and views are right. These racial gatekeepers are enablers of White supremacy. If they were White, they would be racists.

Black people are not a monolith. We have different personalities, opinions, expressions, backgrounds, choices, ethnicities, cultures, languages and so much more that shape our lived experiences. White supremacy and the dehumanisation of our Black identity is a common factor that we all deal with in varying degrees. Some not as bad as others, while others much worse than some. It is astonishing therefore that any Black person or Ethnic Minority would judge institutional racism purely by whether or not they have personally experienced it, deliberately ignoring widespread evidence of racism others experience even when reported by the media. More so, the racial gatekeepers who deny institutional racism today base this on a comparison to the institutional racism of yesterday. Both are one and the same, but today racism manifests differently in overt and covert ways. Making it look like racism against Black people ended with the Civil Rights movements of the 60s and 70s is a farce. There is no doubt in my mind that racial gatekeepers existed during Mandela's struggles with Apartheid or during Martin Luther King and Rosa

Parks' struggles with racial segregation and discrimination. The fact I have never experienced police brutality does not mean it doesn't exist or that it is not evidence of deep-rooted systemic institutional racism. The fact that I have never experienced the racism unleashed on immigrants and asylum seekers does not deny the truth that the British Home Office is institutionally racist.[*]

My resistance to racial gatekeepers is purely about what they stand for, which is the continuation of the status quo and not the erasure of institutional racism and/or dismantling White supremacy. This might be a tad complicated for some who want to claim I hate them: I do not hate anyone. It is not a difference of opinion to prioritise your self-preservation and way of life over an entire community. It is not a difference of opinion to legitimize the dehumanisation and misrepresentation of the Black Identity at the expense of an entire race, thereby giving racists the go-ahead to do so too. Racial gatekeepers are incredibly selfish, self-serving and unrelenting tools of an endemic institutionally racist system that works against all Black people and Ethnic Minorities. It doesn't tell me we want the same thing, like Malcolm X and Martin Luther King Jr, who both wanted social justice for Black people but in different ways. Racial gatekeepers must be resisted because they are part of the problem not the solution.

Let me introduce you to a few racial gatekeepers who cause more damage than is quantifiable. My words might shock or even be controversial, but need to be said. I do not deny their right to share and support racist views or execute actions to legitimise the

---

* Steven Swinford and Oliver Wright, 'Home Office is "institutionally racist", said report into Windrush scandal', *The Times*, 21 February 2020, https://www.thetimes.co.uk/article/home-office-is-institutionally-racist-said-report-into-windrush-scandal-76w9mrw2w.

denial of institutional racism and oppression of Black people, but neither will I deny my right to call them out for what they are – racial gatekeepers.

Following the killing of George Floyd, and during the mass protests across the United States, African American US commentator Candace Owens publicly criticised the #BlackLivesMatter movement for treating him as a 'martyr' and reportedly referred to George Floyd as a horrible human being in a widely shared viral video because of his criminal convictions. She made a point of saying racialised police brutality is a myth. In her words:

'The whole concept of racialized police brutality is a myth. All you have to do is sit down and do basic mathematics to discover the entire narrative we've been sold is a lie. It's a lie. There is no racially targeted police brutality against black Americans. The only thing we're doing disproportionately in America is committing crimes.'*

It would be a waste of time to posit that Candace cannot possibly mean what she says, and even crass, in my humble opinion, to suggest she is saying this for notoriety or for profit. I give all racial gatekeepers the benefit of the doubt by accepting them exactly as they present themselves. Candace believes every single word she uttered to deny police brutality and criticise the Black Lives Matter Movement knowing fully well it will be embraced by those with a far more sinister agenda because her words as a Black woman are

---

* From video clip attached to the article by Alex Miller, 'We need to talk about Candace Owens' problem with George Floyd – and everybody like George Floyd', *Independent*, 10 June 2020, https://www.independent.co.uk/voices/candace-owens-george-floyd-gofundme-crimes-prison-uncle-tom-trump-a9558791.html.

perceived as legitimising them. For a seemingly intelligent woman, she has to know how this could discredit the cause for equality and justice. I don't believe anyone held George Floyd up as a martyr. The truth remains that nothing he had ever done or alleged to have done at the time of his death warranted his killing, which was racially motivated. His manner of death signalled a cry for change and that was right. His death did better at highlighting the insidious nature of institutional racism and police brutality against Black people than Candace Owens could ever fathom. More so, the world will remember George Floyd, the man she called a horrible human being, as a catalyst for positive change and disruption. Only time will tell if Candace Owens will even make a footnote in history.

In England, in response to George Floyd's death, widespread #BlackLivesMatter protests calling for an end to institutional racism in the United Kingdom led Prime Minister Boris Johnson to declare the need for a cross-governmental commission to look at all aspects of race inequality. This was greeted with unstinting criticisms because none of the recommendations of previous race inequality reviews in the last two decades had been implemented by the UK government. These include the MacPherson inquiry* into Stephen Lawrence's death, the David Lammy review† and the Windrush report.‡ As though this was not bad enough, he appointed Munira Mirza, director of the Downing Street policy unit, to set up this Commission. This caused justifiable outrage. Munira Mirza, a British Asian who had publicly stated that institutional racism is a myth,§

---

* https://www.gov.uk/government/publications/the-stephen-lawrence-inquiry.

† https://www.gov.uk/government/publications/lammy-review-final-report.

‡ https://www.gov.uk/government/publications/windrush-lessons-learned-review.

§ Munira Mirza, 'Lammy review: the myth of institutional racism', *Spiked*, 11 September 2017, https://www.spiked-online.com/2017/09/11/lammy-review-the-myth-of-institutional-racism/.

railed against multiculturalism* and called for the dismantling of diversity policies† was not a credible or trustworthy appointment for this role in the views of many in the Black British community. She was a racial gatekeeper in every sense of the word and did not have the confidence of the Black community to lead this race inequality commission, given her stance on the supposed non-existence of institutional racism. Her appointment further demonstrated the Government's lack of intention to eradicate institutional racism. For someone who said 'We should get rid of "tick box" measures that do nothing to address underlying inequality'‡, Munira Mirza ticked the Brown box to execute the Government's bad faith to the Black community. Imagine if a Holocaust denier was appointed to lead a commission on antisemitism or an Islamophobe to head a review into incidences of Islamophobia, and think how Jews and Muslims would react. Munira Mirza was, in effect, a Brown executioner appointed to delegitimise, discredit and deny the structural intersecting inequalities Black people face.

Political figures from an Ethnic Minority background, with significant political influence and power, can undoubtedly be the most egregious kind of racial gatekeepers. Some (not all) use their position and influence to gaslight Ethnic Minorities including their own, which inevitably delays the progress towards race equality. Musa Okwonga's description of the impact of these political figures is apt:

'Racial gatekeeping, put simply, is the assertion that the political figure in question could not possibly be criticised for

---

* Munira Mirza, 'Rethinking race', *Prospect*, 22 September 2020, https://www.prospectmagazine.co.uk/magazine/munira-mirza-multiculturalism-racism.
† Munira Mirza, 'Diversity is Divisive', *Guardian*, 21 November 2006, https://www.theguardian.com/commentisfree/2006/nov/21/diversityhasbecomedivisive.
‡ Ibid.

regressive policies against a particular racially marginalised group, because they themselves are members of that group. [. . .] The racial gatekeeper is a crucial role because it allows a group of white people with racially regressive views to say: "Look at us, we have found a non-white person who agrees with us, our policies therefore do not have racially regressive effects".*

When Home Secretary Priti Patel, who is British Asian, was called out by Members of Parliament from the Labour opposition party for gaslighting, she claimed they were being racist to her because she did not 'conform to their [. . .] stereotypical view of what an Ethnic Minority woman should stand for'.† This is deliberately misleading. The Labour MPs were Black, Asian and Ethnic Minorities, and so could not be accused of being racist to her. The Labour MPs called her out for using her ethnicity and personal experience of racism to delegitimise the existence of institutional racism. These Labour MPs were correct and the evidence of their assertions is proved through Priti Patel's actions, such as legitimising and enforcing foul Government immigration policies against minorities. In addition, there is no stereotypical view of what an Ethnic Minority woman should stand for when no race is a monolith, but there is a standard for any decent human being to stand for and that is not to use their position and influence to deepen racial inequality.

---

* Musa Okwonga, 'The Dangers of Priti Patel's Gatekeeping', *Byline Times*, 3 October 2019, https://bylinetimes.com/2019/10/03/the-dangers-of-priti-patels-racial-gatekeeping/.

† Andrew Woodcock, 'Priti Patel says Labour ethnic minority MPs who accused her of using heritage are "racist"', *Independent*, 28 June 2020, https://www.independent.co.uk/news/uk/politics/priti-patel-labour-mps-ethnic-minority-racism-diane-abbott-a9589671.html.

In light of the incredible sacrifices of key essential workers during the coronavirus pandemic, the United Kingdom was in a perpetual state of thanking NHS workers and carers by clapping for them every Thursday. In the midst of this period of appreciation, Priti Patel introduced a new points-based immigration system, which revealed that immigrant NHS and key essential workers would be classified as too low-skilled to qualify for entry into the UK. This was based on their salaries being small and not on their invaluable skills, which had kept and continues to keep an entire nation functioning. Their skills saved lives during the Covid-19 pandemic.

Priti Patel admitted that, under her new immigration policies, even her own parents, who migrated to the UK in the 1960s, would not qualify for entry into the UK. This shows her as a racial gate-keeper who firmly believes in pulling up the ladder behind her to stop others from enjoying the same benefits she and her family enjoyed. Egregious? Yes. As a British Asian, she ticks the 'Brown box' and gives legitimacy to damaging and regressive policies she executes on behalf of a British government responsible for the 'hostile environment' and the Windrush scandal, and which failed to centre Black, Asian and Ethnic Minorities in its Covid-19 response.

Racial gatekeepers are nothing new and not all have high-profile status. They are progress blockers who man the gate of progress purely for their own self-promotion and self-preservation. It could be a work colleague, classmate or neighbour. I reiterate that their gatekeeping is not about having a difference of opinion – there is nothing wrong with a difference of opinion. It is the positioning of their opinion by actively influencing the staunching of progress that could benefit the wider community of their race that makes them dangerous and their actions an egregious act of betrayal to their race.

'I DON'T SEE COLOUR'

The flipside to accusations against Black people for 'playing the race card' are White people who claim they don't see colour, i.e. they don't see race. These are more often than not well-intentioned White people who want to say the right thing, but what they are actually doing is compounding the problem. In fact, racists use this line too to try to deny their views and acts are objectively racially motivated. I am going to be brutally honest here about this problematic phrase, so White allies and foes alike should get ready to be uncomfortable. Saying you don't see colour is not a compliment!

There is no such thing as not seeing the colour of my skin. You see it and I know you see it. It is false and disingenuous to suggest you don't see a part of me that is most visible to your eye. What you claim not to see is the racial prejudice, racial bias and racialised identity that plagues the Black identity. That too is a lie. You see it. Saying you don't see the dehumanisation, marginalisation, commoditisation and misrepresentation of the Black identity is a privilege you exercise to deny your guilt and complacency for doing nothing or not nearly enough about ending the existence of racism and your benefits therefrom. You say you don't see colour from a place of comfort and forced obliviousness that manifests itself through what you perceive as being a decent person. But as long as you are not actively anti-racist, you are contributing and manifesting racism consciously or sub-consciously.

If you don't see colour, you don't see me. If you don't see me, you don't see the abuse I get because of the colour of my skin. If you think that makes you an ally, it does not. It makes you an appendage. I can't carry you too. When you claim you don't see colour, it means you don't see the beauty, strength and power of my colour. You MUST see my colour – it is part of who I am. The fight is to reject, denounce and unequivocally condemn the Black identity created by White people to feed a false sense of superiority. You must stand with Black people against that, but to stand with us means to acknowledge that no one race is superior to another based on the colour of their skin. For that to happen, you must see our colour and celebrate it with us. Our fight is to proclaim that no longer shall the colour of our skin be used as a barrier against us. The freedom to exercise rights and the right to exercise freedom have long been denied on the premise that an equal value of life and liberty to Black people is the antithesis of White supremacy. Proof of this is in the outcomes of the lived experiences of Black people to date. This is why freedom is a struggle and Black people are still fighting for freedom and rights in the twenty-first century.

Let me give you one simple rule: **See. Our. Colour. But. Don't. Discriminate. Against. It.** This simple rule is difficult for some White people to follow because it means giving up what their way of life is predicated on – race inequality. Institutional racism only perpetuates what White people want and that includes White moderates and allies who, in the words of Martin Luther King Jr:

> 'paternalistically feels that he can set the time-table for another man's freedom; who lives by the myth of time and who constantly advises the Negro to wait until a "more convenient season."' Shallow understanding from people of good will is more frustrating than absolute misunderstanding from people of ill will.'*

Damning words from Martin Luther King Jr which sum up why the phrase 'I don't see colour' is not a sign of allyship but a stumbling block to the freedom of Black people to exercise their rights. Stop running away from the contrived Black identity created by the White race to feed a narrative of false superiority but instead join

---

* Martin Luther King Jr, 'Letter From Birmingham Jail', 16 April 1963.

Black people in confronting and dismantling it. When you don't see colour, it leads to only negative impact for Black people. It fosters the open practice of shutting the doors of progress, acknowledgement and equal outcomes for Black people as has been evident in different industry sectors including the entertainment industry.

This is why the trending *#OSCARSSoWhite* and *#BAFTAS-SoWhite* hashtags led controversial conversations on colour in recent years. Claiming not to see colour has limited the talent pool in many industries and also denied Black people and Ethnic Minorities the space to be publicly recognised for outstanding work they have achieved. When Joaquin Phoenix won the 2020 BAFTA Award for Best Leading Actor, his acceptance speech literally blew the lid off institutional racism in the awards ceremonies and film industry. He spoke of feeling conflicted about winning because many of his colleagues who are deserving don't even get the privilege to be in the room and felt that a message was being sent to people of colour that they are not welcome. He was unequivocal in stating where the responsibility lies in dismantling the current practice that excludes talented people from diverse backgrounds:

> 'I think we send a very clear message to people of colour that "You're not welcome here." That's a message that we are sending to people that have contributed so much to our medium and our industry, and in ways that we benefit from . . . I think that it is the obligation of the people that have created and perpetuate and benefit from a system of oppression to be the ones that dismantle it . . . so that's on us.'*

---

* Adam Wallis, 'Joaquin Phoenix delivers blistering BAFTAs racism speech, says people of colour made to feel "not welcome"', Global News, 4 February 2020, https://globalnews.ca/news/6498842/joaquin-phoenix-baftas-speech-racism/.

Not seeing colour makes any commitment to race diversity insincere and disingenuous. Diversity, like any other form of progression, must be consciously intentional; it must be more than a declaration, it must be a demonstration. Within the film industry, it is the BAFTAs' and Oscars' responsibility to honour, recognise and celebrate the diversity of the demographic. For instance, there were many talented actresses who should have been considered in the leading and supporting actress categories, yet Margot Robbie was nominated twice in the same category at the 2020 BAFTA awards. The likes of Cynthia Erivo in *Harriet*, Lupita Nyong'o in *Us* and Jennifer Lopez in *Hustlers* were not nominated. We are only talking about nominees, not about winning, but how can a demographic win when they are not even nominated? Not seeing colour gaslights Black people and Ethnic Minorities. It is because you see our colour that the barriers to our personal and collective progress exist.

The film *When They See Us* is one of the most powerful television mini-series I have ever watched. It is the true-life crime tragedy of the Central Park Five and was brilliantly directed by African American director Ava DuVernay. I can't write about it without feeling the waves of anger, frustration, tears and anxiety I had when I processed the tragedy unfolding before my eyes and understanding the devastating impact on the lives of five innocent young Black men falsely accused of the violent rape and assault of a White woman. A crime they did not commit. Their only crime was to be Black, the probable cause was their Black identity, and the motive was centuries of racialised stereotypes and tropes used to dehumanise, commoditise, marginalise and misrepresent the Black race. It was a criminal system of injustice against the Black race. This is the colour White people see when they claim they don't see colour or accuse us of 'playing the race card'. *This is why I resist.*

The 'I don't see colour' phrase does not prove lack of prejudice or that race diversity is embraced. It does the exact opposite, because that mindset and behaviour fosters an environment of prejudice and shuts the door on diversity. The purpose of diversity is to ensure that all people have equal access and equal outcomes. If you don't see the differences in people then opportunities and outcomes will only serve the predominant race, gender and sexuality, in this case White, heterosexual, cisgender people. You hurt the cause rather than help the cause by not seeing colour. You are a stumbling block not a bridge when you don't see colour. The phrase 'I don't see colour' is regressive not progressive. To White allies, let me explain this a bit more. 'I don't see colour' does not absolve you of racism and it is not evidence that you are not a racist. Your White privilege is still very much intact and the system built to enforce White supremacy to the detriment of Black people thrives off your colour blindness to racism.

CONCLUDING THOUGHTS . . .

One of the recurring allegations of racial gatekeepers, racists and the anti-woke against anti-racism activists like myself is the lie that we sell oppression and racism to keep Black people down. More often than not, they use Booker T. Washington's 1911 quote to legitimise their point of view:

'There is a class of colored people who make a business of keeping the troubles, the wrongs, and the hardships of the Negro race before the public. Having learned that they are able to make a living out of their troubles, they have grown into the settled habit of advertising their wrongs – partly because they want sympathy and partly because it pays. Some of these people do not want the Negro to lose his grievances, because they do not want to lose their jobs.'*

But this is categorically misapplied to the anti-racism efforts today. We are not disempowering Black people by talking about systemic oppression; we are empowering Black people by breaking down the silence of systemic oppression. It is interesting how detractors often use Don Lemon's June 2014 CNN interview with Morgan Freeman on racism in income inequality in which the esteemed actor said 'if you talk about it [racism] then it exists'† to legitimise their views, or his 2005 interview with Mike Wallace on CBS, in which he was asked how we end racism, to which he responded 'stop talking about it'.‡ I strongly disagree with this point of view. Morgan Freeman does not deny racism exists and has spoken out against it, but unfortunately these quotes can imply that not talking about racism makes it disappear or talking about it is the problem. This is why detractors use it. A perspective akin to Donald Trump's claim that 'If you don't test [coronavirus], you don't have any cases.' There is no merit to such perspectives. A better and more thoughtful response that springs to mind is Meghan Markle in 2020, in a talk with Prince Harry in response to the Black Lives Matter protests, where she said of racism: 'it's not even in the big moments, it's in the quiet moments where racism and unconscious bias lies, hides and thrives'.§ I agree, and this

---

* Booker T. Washington, 'The Intellectuals and the Boston Mob', 1911.

† Morgan Freeman on race and his birthday, CNN, https://edition.cnn.com/videos/bestoftv/2014/06/04/ctn-morgan-freeman-race-birthday.cnn.

‡ Morgan Freeman on Black History Month, https://www.youtube.com/watch?v=Mh8mUia75k8.

§ https://www.independent.co.uk/life-style/royal-family/meghan-markle-prince-harry-black-lives-matter-video-racism-a9603816.html.

is why breaking the silence on racism and oppression is critical. Silence is the killer. It disempowers the oppressed and empowers the oppressor.

I do not have the mindset of someone who is oppressed, but that does not make me blind to the systemic oppression that exists and its discriminatory impact on Black people. All that I have achieved and overcome by the grace of God has been in spite of, not because of, visible and invisible barriers. The fact that I have done so does not make me blind to these barriers. I was not brought up to even remotely think that anything or anyone can stop me being who I want to be. The fact that I am able to do so is not evidence these barriers do not exist. I am not blind to the irrefutable evidence of the discriminatory and disproportionate impact of structural intersecting inequalities on Black people and Ethnic Minorities. More so, my activism is not predicated solely on my lived experience but on the lived experiences of the inequality, injustice and discrimination suffered by others. It is bad enough if just one of us experiences this because, in the words of Martin Luther King Jr, 'injustice anywhere is a threat to justice everywhere.'*

When detractors try to use my education, professional qualifications and accomplishments against me to disprove an oppressive state of institutional racism, they inadvertently prove my point. I am evidence you can overcome some oppressive racial barriers, not evidence it does not exist. Bear in mind that nuances of systemic racism come in layers, some of which I will never experience. However the fact that others have experienced layers of racism I haven't doesn't change my stance that I believe they are worth fighting for. My resistance is against every layer of oppression, inequality and

---

* Martin Luther King Jr, 'Letter From Birmingham Jail', 16 April 1963.

injustice nuanced in the lives of marginalised groups and, when it comes to Black people, the impact of institutional racism can happen to one and all in varying degrees. Ending systemic racism is not up for debate. We must resist the racial gatekeepers, racial micro-aggressors, and racially accusatory attacks of 'playing the race card', which are an attempt to destabilise, delegitimise and discredit the anti-racism efforts.

This is why I resist.

5

CAN I BE ME?

'Not one drop of my self-worth depends on your acceptance of me'*
American record producer, Quincy Jones

As a Black woman, my life is a protest against the objectionable
tropes, negative stereotypes and biases that plague the female Black
identity. The miseducation of the Black woman's identity is a direct
legacy of the dehumanisation of Black women as a consequence
of slavery, colonialism and the enforcement of White supremacy.
Though I would not be born until 1975, the legacy of commoditising, misrepresenting and exploiting the identity of Black women
would be passed down for centuries in varying degrees to influence
how Black women like me are perceived today. This is oppression
and our lived experience. As Black women we are the best expressions of ourselves and as such the most powerful platform and
medium to challenge stereotypical perceptions and definitions used
against us. The aggressors are those who use racial bias, stereotypes
and tropes against us because of the colour of our skin. It begs the
question, can I be me?

---

* https://abcnews.go.com/WN/PersonOfWeek/person-week-quincy-jones/sto-
ry?id=2730571.

If you ask me what my most prominent feature is, the colour of my skin would not come to mind. Not because I am not proud of it but because it is not, and I don't think it should be, my most prominent feature. I equate the colour of my skin to the ability to breathe, walk, run and eat. It is simply a part of me. Being Black does not begin to encapsulate the sum of me, but yet I find I live in a world where the colour of my skin is used to define me, describe me, even set boundaries on who I am meant to be, what I am, judge what I say and cast aspersions on my character. The colour of my skin appears to underpin the perception of some people of me. It doesn't make sense to me that, even though the colour of my skin doesn't guide, define or determine my choices, there are those looking at me from the outside who perceive my choices and actions through their murky and judgemental lens of my race. This is the daily experience in which the 'Black identity' is derived. This contrived perception of Black women puts us in a box we don't belong in and places us in a cage where we are not free to be and do whatever we want.

The miseducation of the Black woman's identity can be deconstructed with these few home truths:

1. Don't you dare call me an 'Angry. Black. Woman' because I am passionate, justifiably angry, biologically female and, yes, of African descent.

2. Don't you dare call me 'Aggressive. Dominant. Bully' because I am visible, have the conviction of my cause, am unapologetically vocal and can assertively defend my opinions.

3. Don't you dare 'Undermine' my excellence and brilliance because of your irrational fear and the unfathomable inferiority complex of your false superiority.

As I have grown older, I find that I now resist these tropes in a different way. I do this by utilising the very narrative used against me, as a Black woman, to upend and challenge the user. If the purpose is to silence me, I do the very opposite and become more vocal. If the purpose is to cast aspersions on my character, I refuse to cower and assertively stand my ground. If the purpose is to diminish my ability, I dig in and let my skills, the product of my work and my passion speak for me. Let me be clear: I do not like the fact that the colour of my skin is being used against me, to describe me and/or define me. It is abhorrent to me that a deliberately misconceived false perception of my Black identity is being used as a standard to judge who I am. However, instead of running or cowering, I am reclaiming the colour of my skin as the means to resist the use of these false definitions and standards against me. *Can I be me?*

The contrived identity of the Black woman positions Black women to suffer violence that is both verbal and physical; visible and invisible, and goes completely ignored while largely erased by society. Black women experience a level of misogynoir, which is the combination of racial and gender bias, that is truly reprehensible. 2020 was the year that, in my view, magnified the grotesque and systemic oppression of the identity of the Black woman. It did not matter if she was rich or poor, celebrity or not, and it was irrespective of socio-economic background; as long as she was of Black descent, she was subjected to the prejudice that results from a dehumanising and contrived Black identity. From the constant barrage of racially undertoned abuse targeted at **Meghan Markle**, Duchess of Sussex, to the failure to charge the police officers who killed **Breonna Taylor** in her home ten weeks before George Floyd's killing and widespread protests; from years of erasing the experience of police brutality and domestic violence towards Black women to the horrific and amplified spike of violence against Black Trans women, including **Riah Milton** and **Dominique Rem'mie Fells**, the struggle to end the dehumanisation of Black women has too long been invisible and ignored. It is time to break down the walls of silence and fight the violence against Black women. *This is why I resist.*

As though being stigmatised for being Black is not enough, the shade of my Black skin tone is also the subject of discrimination. Known as colourism, this discrimination divides Black women who are already marginalised for their race and gender by bestowing preferential treatment to lighter-skinned Black women. This discrimination is inevitably to the detriment of darker-skinned Black women. The obsession with lighter skin is because of its proximity to Whiteness and the inherited prejudice from legacies of slavery and colonialism that dehumanised the Black skin tone as inferior. Colourism is a double-edged sword – it is racism reproduced by White Supremacy to further prejudice Blacks against Blacks; and it is the Stockholm Syndrome of racism as it permeates the Black communities it subjugates so that, even within them, lighter-skinned Black women are treated with preference. Oscar-winning actress **Lupita Nyong'o** described colourism as 'the daughter of racism', further explaining it 'rewards lighter skin over darker skin.'* What colourism does is as physically, emotionally and mentally destructive to a Black woman's self-esteem and sense of self as the erasure of her physical, emotional and mental experience of abuse. Colourism is oppression and its use as a tool of preference for lighter-skinned Black women, in media, politics, schools, modelling and many other areas, inevitably stifles opportunities and outcomes for darker-skinned Black women, and pits Black women against each other over the shade of their skin tone. This is White Supremacy. Today, shades of Black skin tones are still racialised, prejudiced against and used to define the worth and beauty of darker-skin toned Black women. I unequivocally reject this. *This is why I resist. Can I be me?*

---

* BBC News, 8 October 2019, https://www.bbc.co.uk/news/entertainment-arts-49976837.

THE 'ANGRY BLACK WOMAN'

This stereotypical trope against Black women as loud, vocal, dominant, angry, aggressive, opinionated, threatening, hostile and bullies is an insidious camouflage. This trope has only one purpose – to demean, dehumanise and silence Black women. Be passionate and you are perceived as angry. Be passionate and vocal, you're perceived as opinionated. Be passionate, vocal and direct, you're perceived as aggressive. Add all those together and you're perceived as dominant. Being able to strongly assert and defend your own opinions, you're called a bully. God help us if we are justifiably angry and respond in no uncertain terms to attacks, if we did we would be perceived as threatening. Where exactly do we draw the line?

Let me make a clear distinction here. There are women from other races and ethnicities, be they White or Brown, who experience similar labels being applied to them. But understand that no other race suffers from the same consequences as Black women do from this negative trope. It negatively impacts Black women in every sphere of life from the workplace, schools, communities, business and all the way to government. There is no safe space from this trope for Black women unless we face it head on, resist it on a daily basis (as we do!) and literally assert our definition of who we are as Black women. The only way to deconstruct the miseducation of the Black woman's identity is through resistance. The 'angry Black woman' trope is very much about putting Black women in a box. Be under no illusion that though this trope is predominantly used by some White people against Black women, please understand it is also used by a minority of non-Black Ethnic Minorities. When White-led tropes are used by non-Black Ethnic Minorities against Black women, it offers those White people some legitimacy, because it is perceived not to have any racial bias. This is wrong. It *does* have racial bias by

White people and prejudice from the non-Black Ethnic Minorities. This 'angry Black woman' trope is a form of bullying. It is basically saying to Black women that you cannot conduct yourself and are found lacking if said 'expression' falls short of their Eurocentric standards. Note that these so-called standards were not established *by* Black people *for* Black people but *by* White people *for* Black people so, in short, we are being set up to fail.

A good example of the use of the 'angry Black woman' trope were the headlines against **Serena Williams** in 2018 following her controversial US Open loss.* She was portrayed as an 'angry Black woman' for being outraged by the referee's decision to find her in breach of allegedly receiving handsignals from her coach which constituted a code violation for coaching and was given a penalty point for breaking her racquet. Her anger was no different from any other professional in similar circumstances but she was punished for it. When Black women push back on injustice and the wrong done against us, we are immediately called aggressive, angry, domineering and loud. It is easier for them to say this than face their hypocrisy and racism. How dare we push back or express anger at an attack on our integrity? There was absolutely nothing wrong with Serena being vocal and direct about the sexist decision of the umpire in a sport where male players have not received such harsh penalties for similar conduct. I would have done exactly the same thing. Applying the negative trope against her was deliberate. It lacked any under-standing of her justifiable anger and tried to shut down the root of why she was angry. Even worse in my opinion is that the use of the trope was a demeaning way to police her behaviour and judge her anger as falling short of 'standards'. This is completely wrong and outrageous. Nobody should tell you how to express yourself.

---

* Ritu Prasad, 'Serena Williams and the trope of the "angry black woman"', BBC News, 11 September 2018, https://www.bbc.co.uk/news/world-us-canada-45476500.

This has also been my experience. I can recall, for example, an altercation with another activist who is Muslim Asian which escalated. She blamed me unreasonably for a decision by an external organisation that had nothing to do with me. Yet she verbally attacked my integrity on the issue and did so in the view of other activists in the group. I didn't want to get angry but was irritated and told her in no uncertain terms she was crossing the line with her accusations and not to piss me off. She immediately called me aggressive and threatening. It was the second time this activist had called me aggressive. I could see exactly the meaning behind her words. It was an attempt to shut down my right to defend myself against character assassination and my right to express my anger at the indignity I was experiencing. Though she started the altercation by confronting me, I was deemed the aggressor for being vocal and direct in refuting her accusations. Apparently using words like 'don't piss me off' and 'crossing the line' were not acceptable standards, but her barbed accusations were. What was quite shocking was that she compared me telling her 'not to piss me off' to a White supremacist who had attacked her family when she was younger. Imagine for a second how shaken I was to be compared to heinous and vile racist White supremacists, who exploited, maimed, killed and dehumanised my race for centuries. The lack of thought as to what kind of trauma this could trigger for me and the use of such inflammatory words to cause pain were ignored because of another racial stereotype that perceives me as a 'strong Black woman'. Let me break this down for you. You see, our perceived strength as Black women is feared and our power of expression is silenced out of fear, yet we are meant to endure any kind of abuse because of the strength they fear. We can't win for losing. This problematic racial stereotype of the 'strong Black woman', discussed in further detail in this chapter, is very much interwoven with the 'angry Black woman' stereotype.

The bottom line is that using the 'angry Black woman' trope is far easier to feed a negative narrative about Black women and camouflage the user's fear of us. When people don't like you, they will use a negative trope and what is perceived as rational narrative to camouflage their dislike of you. This trope not only exists but persists in the current political, economic and socio-cultural spheres of our lives and continually tries to box us in. It is an attempt to take away our power of expression, power of opinion and power of authenticity. It is as though we don't have the right to be passionate, have an opinion or be angry if the circumstances call for it. Not all Black women are loud or vocal and direct. It isolates the visible and vocal Black woman by trying to crush her voice because she is seen as behaving badly. Black women who are not as vocal or visible are perceived to accept the Eurocentric standards imposed on us and seen to conform to what is expected of them. The moment a Black woman speaks her own mind, expresses her authenticity and resists the status quo, every negative trope and stereotype against Black women, she is a problem.

I am assertive in my opinions, behaviour and body language, all of which are quite different from aggression, which is to be physically intimidating and violent. I refuse to change who I am, my authentic way of expression, to suit another person's view of how I should be or behave. I resist this imposition on my right to be me. This does not prevent me from self-assessing, taking on board constructive feedback and personally developing in areas where I am a work in progress. However, I reject being disproportionately discriminated against by the use of definitions, assumptions, perceptions, bias, prejudice and the like used to mischaracterise me.

The miseducation of the Black woman's identity starts with a commitment from White and non-Black Ethnic Minorities to stop projecting their fear and to start engaging with Black women in a productive way, with emotional intelligence, with empathy and collaboration. Stop projecting your insecurity when you lack the ability to defend your opinions against the opinion of a Black woman or inability to defend your utterances against the utterances of a Black woman. Just because you lack what it takes to stand up to the scrutiny of a Black woman with a difference of opinion does not mean you are being bullied. Be it a debate, discourse, difference of opinion in any format (including an argument), assigning a label or trope to a Black woman because you fear and/or dislike her is just plain lazy and wrong. I don't care if you are White or non-Black Ethnic Minority, it is rooted in racism, racial bias and racial prejudice. *This is why I resist.*

THE 'STRONG BLACK WOMAN'

'When feminists acknowledge in one breath that black women are victimized and in the same breath emphasize their strength, they imply that though black women are oppressed they manage to circumvent the damaging impact of oppression by being strong – and that is simply not the case. Usually, when people talk about the "strength" of black women they are referring to the way in which they perceive black women coping with oppression. They ignore the reality that to be strong in the face of oppression is not the same as overcoming oppression, that endurance is not to be confused with transformation.'*

bell hooks

This racial bias dressed up as a compliment is in no way complimentary. It is a stereotypical trope deceptively used to cause untold

---

* bell hooks, *Ain't I a Woman: Black Women and Feminism*, South End Press, 1981.

damage to the identity of Black women, and it is particularly draining and exhausting. The strength we are perceived to have is used against us because White society perceives us to be strong in the face of oppression, persecution and hardship. The result of this, in a society entrenched with institutional racism, is to pile on more hardship with utter disregard for the negative impact on our quality of life and choice. It appears there is an unwritten rule that Black women are more durable to suffering or more physically capable of taking on oppression and hardship compared to their female White counterparts. The justification for this racial bias is a direct legacy of the transatlantic slave trade and hence the intersectionality of structural inequalities Black women face today.

This stereotype and resulting racial bias were not created by Black women but by White society as a suppressant of the Black woman – let's call it a backhanded compliment. Think about it – who benefits from this bias? Definitely not Black women. If the Black woman's identity is as a superwoman who never complains, is always in control, no crack in the façade and unrelenting, she is effectively silenced. Her authenticity is compromised and her image is dehumanised to fit this stereotypical trope. Are Black women strong? Yes. Resilient? Yes. Hardworking? Yes. Vulnerable? Yes. Emotional? Yes. Get Tired? Yes. And so much more. There is no competition or choice between breaking down in tears and living to overcome another day – Black women have to do both. This is how Black women persevere, resist and overcome structural intersecting inequalities they experience.

bell hooks explains that White people ignore the reality between coping with oppression and overcoming oppression, but I do not think White society even recognises that we do overcome. When faced with Black working- or middle-class people getting good jobs or going to elite schools, some White people are quite surprised and demonstrate the blissful ignorance that their White privilege extends to them when they are not doubted about what school they are going to or what job they have. I think the 'strong Black woman' trope brands the Black woman's identity with endurance of levels of oppression and hardship White society cannot endure. This is why, no matter how fawned over the 'strong Black woman' is, no White woman is ready to swap places with a Black woman for even one day.

This racial bias victimises Black women not as the superwoman one would think but as a woman of hardship. The truth is that the perception of this strength is not admired but expected, as the legacy of female slaves enduring hardship, pitied not empathised with, and this strength is not attractive. Surely if it was superwoman strength, every White woman would be vying to be a 'strong Black woman'? But that is not the case, so you know this contrived identity of the 'strong Black woman' offers no advantage to the identity of Black women and I don't believe it is meant to. In an interview with *Essence*, actress **Taraji P. Henson** calls it out as the trope it is:

'It came as a thing to empower us but then, as years go on, we've been ignored because of that very statement. It dehumanized us, our pain; it belittles our tears. We're supposed to be able to watch our brothers, sons and fathers be murdered in the streets. But we can take it because we're "strong." We can deal with it. And that's just not true. I have issues with titles like that and "black girl magic" because we're not fairies. We don't magically rebound from our pain. We hurt and suffer just like others.'*

---

* Jasmine Grant, 'Taraji P. Henson On Why The "Strong Black Woman" Identity Damages Us', *Essence*, 6 July 2020, https://www.essence.com/lifestyle/health-wellness/essence-wellness-house/taraji-p-henson-explains-why-the-strong-black-woman-identity-at-essence-wellness-house/.

The racial bias also contributes to the higher Black maternal and pregnancy-related deaths when expectant Black mothers are not taken seriously, listened to or given any empathy in their care because they are 'strong Black women'. In Britain, there is a five-fold higher mortality rate for Black women compared with White women, while in America pregnancy-related deaths among Black women are three to four times higher than among White women.[*] A significant contribution to this is the centuries-old trope that Black women don't experience pain like White women. This is utter pejorative nonsense to justify the inhumane treatment of Black women and further health disparities and inequalities in favour of White women.

But this racial bias about the pain threshold of Black women has historical basis in the work of America's most famous gynaecologist, James Marion Sims, known as the father of modern gynaecology. His methods, discoveries and breakthroughs were as a result of experimenting on Black enslaved women without anaesthesia. He is credited for the method to repair vesicovaginal fistula, the first successful gallbladder surgery and artificial insemination. All this at the expense of at least ten enslaved women, treated without anaes-thesia between 1846 and 1849, one of whom was seventeen-year-old enslaved Black woman, **Anarcha Westcott**, who underwent at least thirty unconsented experimental surgeries without anaesthesia for vesicovaginal fistula and rectovaginal fistula as a result of unhealed tears in her vagina and rectum after giving birth. She also suf-fered from a severe case of rickets, a condition not uncommon among slaves, because of severe malnutrition and lack of vitamin D. This coupled with vesicovaginal fistula and rectovaginal fistula

---

* Emma Kasprzak, 'Why are Black mothers at more risk of dying?', BBC, 11 April 2019, https://www.bbc.co.uk/news/uk-england-47115305.

made bowel movements painful, led to infections and bad odour, which often meant being ostracised from other people. It was Black women like Anarcha who were forced to undergo experimental procedures without medication and, once successful, surgeons like James Marion Sims would provide the same treatment to White women. History shows that James Marion Sims opened a women's hospital in New York in the 1850s and provided these treatments, no longer experiments, to White women, but now with the anaesthesia he had denied his Black patients.

Some defend Sims' actions on the basis that he was a product of his time, but this is racist apologist nonsense. Those experiments were unconsented by enslaved women who were seen as property with no rights, and were inhumanely painful. I have birthed three children with a significant tear in the first birth that led to third-degree stitching from my vaginal opening to my anal sphincter. It scarred me. I recall saying to the doctor and nurses as I was sewn up that I could feel the needle threading through my skin and I was in pain. I was ignored and nothing additional was given to me to stop the pain. I did not know then what I know now.

I can only imagine how excruciating it must have been for Anarcha Westcott and those enslaved Black women. The lack of anaesthesia was inhumane. It would not have impacted her treatment but would have given Anarcha and these enslaved women better care. Their suffering was made worse with more suffering because they were perceived to be stronger than White women. James Sims showed utter contempt for the lives and suffering of Black women. His actions were unacceptable then as they would be today, regardless of the pioneering discoveries in medicine credited to him.

James Sims' actions are some of those that contributed to the institutional racist treatment of medical care given to Black people today. For example, a nurses' textbook titled *Nursing – A Concept*

Based Approach to Learning published as recently as 2017 by Pearson Education held racist and prejudiced views in the medical care and treatment of Black people and Ethnic Minorities. It is no longer in circulation but had included non-evidence-based culturally insensitive prejudiced views, such as:

> 'About "Blacks": Blacks often report higher pain intensity than other cultures. They believe suffering and pain are inevitable. About "Arabs/Muslims": Pain is considered a test of faith. Muslim clients must endure pain as a sign of faith in return for forgiveness and mercy. About "Hispanics": Hispanics may believe that pain is a form of punishment and that suffering must be endured if they are to enter heaven.'*

I am going to correct the false framing of history and say James Sims is not the father of modern-day gynaecology, rather it is Anarcha Westcott who is the mother of modern-day gynaecology.

The repeated racial bias strips the female Black identity of being capable of emotion, such as 'we don't feel pain, shed tears or get hurt'. This racial bias fails to acknowledge centuries of racial discrimination that present-day Black women still face, and that what is perceived as strength is actually the daily coping mechanism of dealing with discrimination in its varying forms.

Today, Black women have reclaimed their identity and redefined what it means to be a strong Black woman by rejecting the false depiction of a superwoman who has a penchant for enduring oppression as a way of life. Our strength recognises there is strength

---

* Steve Ford, '"Racist" nursing textbook pulled after criticism on social media', *Nursing Times*, 26 October 2017, https://www.nursingtimes.net/news/education/racist-nursing-textbook-pulled-after-criticism-on-social-media-26-10-2017/.

in trial, tribulations and triumph. It acknowledges us as overcomers not the overcome and recognises us as transformative not stagnant. When Black women say 'I am a strong Black woman', it is not just words of empowerment but words of powering up. These words are a manifestation of the truth of our lived experiences, good and bad, without any baggage of the trope. It becomes an affirmation and proclamation of enduring strength that is human, humane and humbling.

JUST SAY MY NAME

My name is Adéṣolá, shortened to Ṣola, which I prefer to spell as Shola because the 'ṣ' is the 'sh' sound. In the Yoruba language it means 'crowned with wealth' or 'this crown makes wealth' as my father explained to me. Our names matter. Say. My. Name. Black-sounding names like African or African American names for example, face discrimination either because they are seen as difficult and unpronounceable or, in some quarters, they are mocked as a 'ghetto'-sounding name. This racial discrimination is not reserved for schools or the workplace but also manifests itself in the daily experiences of Black people, even though there are laws against such racial discrimination. It has led to some Black people anglicising their first and/or last names so as to fit in, and that includes generations of Black people before my generation. They felt they had to change their names to appear less ethnic and Whiter, in order to fit into a society entrenched with racial bias and discrimination towards Black and ethnic-sounding names.

I don't get easily offended when some people can't pronounce my African name, be it my first name, 'Shola', or my surname, 'Mos-Shogbamimu'. I get that my surname can be a challenge for those not used to it or those seeing it for the first time, but who don't wish to cause offence by mispronouncing it. I honestly get it. But it is disrespectful when some don't even bother to try to pronounce my name and it is offensive when my name becomes a way of expressing their bigotry and *otherism*. Some say 'Oh, your name is a bit difficult'. No. My name is not difficult at all. If you took the time to engage with the alphabetical phonetic training you were taught at primary school, you should be able to read and pronounce my name with ease. If you can say Schwarzenegger, Swarovski, Scherzinger and so on, you should be able to say my name. We need to afford people's names the respect we expect for ourselves, especially when the names look, sound and read different from ours.

While 'Mos-Shogbamimu' is not my birth name but my married name, nevertheless I own it and it is part of who I am. It is not unusual when I go to speak at events, take part in a TV or radio interview or even in the workplace that someone will ask 'how do I pronounce your name?' I am not offended to be asked and usually say to them: 'give it a go'. They then read it, and some get it with ease while others trip over their tongue saying it too fast or missing a letter or two. The one that often gets them is saying 'Shag' instead of 'Shog'. Even at meetings in the workplace, where everyone else in the meeting is introduced by their full name, when it comes to me, I'm introduced as Shola. There is no attempt to even say my full name. For the longest time, I was quiet about this. Though I was not deeply offended, I found it irksome and, at a certain level, quite disrespectful, because my name was not being accorded the same respect as others'. The exclusion is subtle and non-visible, but done in a public space, because there are always other people present. Be it on a conference call or physical meeting, the effect is always the same. When you disrespect my name, treat it with contempt or dismiss it by not pronouncing it in full, because it is inconvenient to do so, you are messing with my Black identity. The immediate impact of it is embarrassment and it is the speaker who is embarrassed not me. Even worse are those who ought to be embarrassed but don't express any discomfort at their disrespect. White-sounding names are never treated this way but Black and Ethnic Minority-sounding names are.

It has led to many Africans anglicising their surnames or choosing a different first name to make others feel comfortable with their name. *This is why I resist.* I refuse to swap the power and authenticity of my African name for an anglicised version that does not represent me. When it comes to my identity making others feel comfortable or not, it is not my priority. It occurred to me one day that I had to address this head on and I did this by taking control of the narrative at the moment the speaker flounders. Regardless of who it is or where it is, I either make them say my name, correct them when they say my name wrong or publicly call them out for excluding my name. A good example was in October 2018 when I was a panel speaker at the launch of the British Council comprehensive report on Women Power Politics. The launch took place at the Houses of Parliament with a female Member of Parliament as the Chair of the panel.

According to our pre-event brief, she would introduce each panellist and invite them to answer opening questions. I was the fourth panel speaker to be introduced and I noticed the preceding three speakers were introduced by their full names while giving a brief synopsis of their bios. However, when it came to me, I was introduced as 'Dr Shola Mos'. She didn't pause or even try to say my surname. As she was about to say something about my bio, I interrupted her and said very clearly: 'Say my name'. I looked at her and repeated 'Say my name' in front of the audience. She tried to pronounce it, I corrected her and nodded for her to continue with her introduction. The room was silent, but in that moment I had taken hold of the narrative and dealt with this subtle but visible exclusion. So rather than wait for someone else to include me, I did it myself. Plus, if there was any embarrassment, it was the Chair's not mine, because I am not embarrassed by my name. Hopefully this was a teachable moment for her.

As Chair, she should have prepared beforehand to accord me the same level of respect as she did the other speakers. Introducing me to an audience, most of whom will be meeting me for the first time, is an important part of their introduction to my identity as a Black woman. I recall that, at the start of my presentation, I posed the elephant-in-the-room question to the audience: 'Why am I the only Black person in the room?' Silence. I challenged the room and organisers of the event with my observation that we can't possibly start to expect change in equal representation in politics when, in events such as this, there is no equal representation. From my recollection, there were two or three other Ethnic Minorities present, though I was the only Black person, and the audience was predominantly White. This absence of a diverse audience is just as exclusionary as the absence of thought in pronouncing African or Black-sounding names.

Far less subtle and more visible are those who deliberately attack our Black identity by treating our names as different and unpronounceable with the sole intention of telling us we do not belong. Social media has become the magnetic conduit for communicating such deliberate abuse and discrimination. I have experienced quite a number of such attacks on social media and here is a good example. In response to my tweet on 19 October 2019, talking about the People's Vote march I had participated in with London Mayor Sadiq Khan and thousands of others, I got a tweet from Janice Atkinson, a self-described conservative Brexiteer. She immediately went for my name, not my protest against Brexit. She sought to draw me out as a nobody with 'Who are you?' and, to single me out as not belonging because my name isn't White-sounding, followed it with 'How do we pronounce your name?' Note how the distinction of '*we*' immediately connotes otherism; she is saying 'you are not one of us and you don't belong here'. Furthermore, the emphasis on 'pronounce your name' is meant to exclude me by suggesting my name is difficult and unpronounceable. I took hold of the narrative and put her racist bigotry in its place by informing her that 'if you can't read my name, you're an illiterate. If you can't pronounce my name, you're lazy'. I am British born and very proud of my African name. It is so important to our Black identity to resist any form of oppression. Exclusion and otherisms are forms of oppression. There is power in my name. It should be respected, as I ought to be respected. White-sounding names are not better, stronger or of more value than my name. To treat my name as less than valuable is to say I am not valuable. I totally reject that. I wear my African name as a badge of honour. It is different from others and I think that is a good thing. My name is not common because I am uncommon. It is unique and stands out, just like me. I will take pride in my name, the same one you find difficult to pronounce. I take pride in the fact that I am different and called to be different. 'Say my name' is a powerful way to take back control of the narrative of our identity as Black women. ***This is why I resist.***

LEAVE MY HAIR ALONE

The discrimination against Afro-textured ethnic hairstyles is real. Black women are marginalised and discriminated against because of our hair texture and hairstyles. It is not a figment of our imagination nor is the discrimination we face justified in the workplace or schools on the grounds of 'professional standard'. This 'professional standard' is founded on a Eurocentric sense of hair beauty that is part of the history of White supremacy and continues to enforce it.

Policing our hair is another legacy of slavery and colonialism that demonstrates the continual dehumanisation of the Black identity. It is racial bias and discrimination of our hair because of the colour of our skin and an egregious attempt to make our natural hair texture and ethnic hairstyles look ugly by Eurocentric standards in order to enforce White supremacy. Even our hair must be subjugated by the inferiority complex of a false White superiority. Black identity, subjugation, power and freedom are intertwined in our Afro hairstyles and texture. Policing Black hair is symptomatic of institutional racism in Britain and America. It is racist.

In America, the States of New York and California have banned racial hair discrimination against hairstyles such as braids, Bantu knots, twists and locs. It is treated as a breach of human rights and punishable under the law. California's CROWN Act (abbreviated for Create a Respectful and Open Workplace for Natural Hair) deems 'hair' to be representative of race and as such updated the definition of Race, in the California Fair Employment and Housing Act and the California Education Code, to be 'inclusive of traits historically associated with race, including, but not limited to, hair texture and protective hairstyles.'* The CROWN Act prohibits grooming policies that are deceptively race neutral but objectively have a disproportionate negative impact on people of colour, particularly Black people. The New York City Commission on Human Rights describes 'natural hair, treated or untreated hairstyles, such as locs, cornrows, twists, braids, Bantu knots, fades, Afros, and/or the right to keep hair in an uncut or untrimmed state' as hairstyles that are not to be subjected to discrimination.† Though many White women, including female students, wear hair extensions and dye

---

* Calif. Government Code § 212.1 and Calif. S.B. 188.

† NYC Admin. Code § 8107.

their hair different colours, they do not experience the bias or discrimination that could cost them their right to an education or job, which African American and Black British people including children have experienced. There is an unequal treatment that is overt and racist which these Black children experience at a young age because of prejudiced mindsets that deem ethnic hairstyles to be sub-standard in comparison to Eurocentric standards. This is White supremacy.

In January 2020, eighteen-year-old **DeAndre Arnold** was suspended from school at Barbers Hill High School in Texas for dreadlocks he started growing in the seventh grade and was facing missing his high-school prom and graduation. In the same month at the same school, sixteen-year-old **Kaden Bradford** was suspended for the length of his dreadlocks. In December 2018, **Andrew Johnson**, from New Jersey, was made to cut his dreadlocks by a White referee who called it unnatural and gave him 90 seconds to either cut his dreadlocks off or forfeit participating in his school's wrestling match. He gave this young boy 90 seconds to choose between his Black identity or let his school mates down. This was a public humiliation and racist discrimination. Andrew (known as Drew) was filmed with his dreadlocks cut and the video went viral, causing public outrage leading to the referee being suspended from officiating for two years. In September 2018, **Faith Fennidy** was expelled from Christ the King middle school in Louisiana because her braids were considered unacceptable under the school code. Footage of her sobbing uncontrollably as she packed her bags went viral, also causing public outrage. She had been wearing similar braids for at least two years at school before it changed its policy. In August 2018, six-year-old **Clinton Stanley Jr** was denied entry on his first day of school at Book's Christian Academy in Florida and was sent home because his hair did not conform to the school handbook standard, which did not permit dreadlocks. In 2017, twin sisters **Mya** and **Deana Cook** served detention because their school, Mystic Valley Regional Charter School in Massachusetts, bans hair extensions in its dress code, deeming them distracting. The school officials determined Mya and Deana's braids violated school policy. There is no equivalent prohibition under English law that bans policies and practices that discriminate against ethnic natural hair-styles, particularly of Black people. Employees have sued current and former employers for hair discrimination and Black British children of Black or mixed heritage are excluded from school for dreadlocks, braids, Afros and fades. Current legislation in the UK does not go far enough to protect Black people. Employers and schools can have their own dress code policy and impose standards about acceptable hairstyles but must demonstrate real business need for the policy and that it is proportionate on its impact. This is utterly inadequate when what determines 'standard' does not recognise the legitimacy of Afro hair and hairstyles.

In 2016, fourteen-year-old **Chyna Cowie-Sullivan** was told by her school teacher at Fulston Manor School in Kent to remove her braids because it was an extreme hairstyle and against school policy. Her mother led a 30,000+ petition against the school before it saw the error of its ways and changed its school policy. In 2018, twelve-year-old **Chikayzea Flanders** was told to cut off his dreadlocks or leave Fulham Boys School in London because it did not comply with the school's uniform and appearance policy. Legal action launched by his mother and funded by the Equality and Human Rights Commission led to a reversal of the school's decision. The mother's campaign was on the basis that Chikayzea's dreadlocks were fundamental to his Rastafarian beliefs and must be exempt from the school policy. In 2019, six-year-old **Josiah Sharpe** told his parents he did not want to be Black any more after he was banned from the playground at breaktimes and eventually sent home from school for his 'extreme' haircut, which was a fade. The Summerhill Primary Academy in Sandwell, England, said it did not comply with school policy and that he would be allowed to return when his hair grew back to what the school deemed an appropriate length. In 2020, **Ruby Williams** won £8,500 in an out-of-court settlement following legal action against The Urswick School in East London, where she had been repeatedly sent home because of her natural Afro hair, which was deemed to be against uniform policy. These experiences clearly show that hair discrimination is about control and power. *This is why I resist.*

BLACK IDENTITY IN THE WORKPLACE

The workplace can be a cesspool of Black identity mischarac-terisation and exclusion. I recall, during a senior stakeholders meeting at a global financial institution I worked at, a White senior relationship manager described the deal he was seeking to onboard with a client as coming from 'Deep Dark Africa'. I was mid-level compared to the seniority of positions represented in the room, which were White male, one of whom was the overall head of the Treasury business covering Europe, Middle East and Africa. My reaction to the use of the words 'Deep Dark Africa' was immediate. As soon as he uttered the words, I faced him and repeated each word with double emphasis and said nothing else. It was all I could manage to say in that moment. There was no doubt in my meaning that it was offensive. The meeting wrapped up and I left.

Within a short time, the Head of Treasury business came to my floor to personally apologise and I received a written apology from the senior relationship manager via email. What was interesting was the response of my White female manager, who laughed when she heard about the incident and told me she explained to the Head of Treasury that 'Shola is not like that; she's not offended that way'. I remember how surprised she was when I corrected her and said 'Deep Dark Africa' was offensive. Referring to the African continent as deep and dark has a historical racist connotation that attributes savagery and ignorance to its people. The derogatory use of these words still has the same impact and meaning as it did back in the 1800s. Sometimes applying deductive reasoning by analysing the context in which certain terms are used should give a hint (however faint or strong) of the purpose of the term. While I can give them the benefit of the doubt, they lose all credibility if, once corrected, they fail to apply what they have learned, fail to share that learning with others and/or fail to apply a smidgen of deductive reasoning to other terms in the bank of vocabulary or future terms they come across. The fact it is used colloquially in the office space does not make it okay or acceptable.

The fact that our African or Black-sounding names, which are part of our Black identity and culture, can be used as a barrier against us in the workplace is part of the problem in dehumanising and marginalising our Black identity, despite legislation and policies sanctioning against it. Researchers at Oxford University's Nuffield College Centre for Social Investigation (CSI) shared the shocking results of discrimination against Ethnic Minorities in job applications, particularly Black people and South Asians, for whom they revealed there had been no sign of progress for the past fifty years. The researchers demonstrated the levels of discrimination against job applicants from Ethnic Minority backgrounds by doing the following:

'We made fictitious applications to nearly 3,200 real jobs, randomly varying applicants' minority background, but holding their skills, qualifications and work experience constant. On average, nearly one in four applicants from the majority group (24%) received a callback from employers. The job search effort was less successful for ethnic minorities who, despite having identical CVs and cover letters, needed to send 60% more applications in order to receive as many callbacks as the majority group.'*

People do not leave their prejudice, bias or racism at home when they come to the workplace. Sometimes it is concealed and at other times quite overt. Oftentimes the use of colloquial terms in the mainstream that have a historical derogatory emphasis against Black people are watered down as 'unconscious bias' or ignorance. This is unacceptable. There are people who will genuinely not know or understand the history behind certain terms. While I am prepared to give them the benefit of the doubt, it is quite exhausting for Black people to continually bear the responsibility of doing the unpicking and unlearning for White people. When do we get a break from carrying a responsibility that is not ours to bear? If generations of White people had done a better job in educating the next generation, learning from the errors and legacy of slavery, my generation would not be left with the responsibility of picking up the pieces.

---

* 'New CSI research reveals high levels of job discrimination faced by ethnic minorities in Britain', Centre for Social Investigation, 18 January 2019, http://csi. nuff.ox.ac.uk/?p=1299.

CONCLUDING THOUGHTS ...

As much as I seek to educate about the miseducation of the Black woman's identity, I would very much like readers, particularly White people, to broaden their interpretation of my words and place themselves within them where possible, in order to sense what it must be like to have to deal with these multiple racial biases, stereotype and discrimination against our identity. These are barriers – verbal or non-verbal and overt or covert – that we have to deal with constantly. They shape our lived experiences. We do not have the luxury of being hampered by them one at a time, as multiple incidents can occur in a single day. This is what we have to deal with so that the narrative for White supremacy can continue to thrive at the expense of our life and liberty. The true narrative of the Black woman's identity is one of honour, celebration and respect. There must be a positive cultural shift towards this as Black women stand unequivocal in our truth. That cultural shift starts now.

This is why I resist.

6

DOES MY AFRO-VISIBLE FEMINISM THREATEN YOU?

'It is not our differences that divide us. It is our inability
to recognize, accept, and celebrate those differences.' *
**American writer, feminist, womanist, librarian,
and civil rights activist, Audre Lorde**

I love feminism! The power of our sisterhood, a unifier of women
from diverse cultural and socio-economic backgrounds, faiths, affili-
ations, politics, abilities, sexuality, age and so much more. With
feminism, we are all different parts of one body in solidarity, strength
and sisterhood. It is and can truly be a powerful sense of belonging.
Feminism should not ignore what is different about us but celebrate
our differences. If you stand for equal political, economic and social
rights for women, then you're a feminist. I find that when I celebrate
other women, I celebrate me. By celebrating them, the me of today
recognises in their success that, if they can do it, I can do it too. I am
celebrating the me of today who aspires to be the me of tomorrow,
and I'm celebrating the me of tomorrow because she is inspired by
all these badass women I celebrate. There are so many women I

---

* Audre Lorde, 'Age, Race, Class and Sex: Women Redefining Difference', 1980.

genuinely admire and respect, because, in feminism, I can stand in solidarity with sisters of all creeds, races, faiths, sexualities, abilities, ages and diverse backgrounds.

However, I have found, in my experience, that the very spaces in British and American feminist movements that are meant to be for Black women are monopolised by White women. They claim to 'create' these spaces for us to justify our presence and that, if it was not for them, Black voices would not be heard. I am fortunate to be part of multiple campaigns and grassroots activism in the women's rights movement as well as working with some really incredible campaigners and activists from all walks of life and backgrounds, so I can say for a fact that most White feminists I have worked with are *fellow feministas*, with whom I share a common goal in solidarity and sisterhood. But I have met and campaigned with a few White feminists who have exemplified every trait of a White supremacist mindset and used their White privilege when they felt their spaces were being dominated by Black women.

Representation of Black women in the British and American feminist movements is vital and necessary. The women's rights and feminist movement cannot claim to be inclusive and diverse if we are not representative of the political, economic and social rights of women we seek to uphold. But what I find particularly surprising is the lack of direct application of intersectionality in the collective experience of feminist activism. As a Black feminist, it is unfathomable that the multiple representations I embody are not understood or that the inequalities Black women experience are compartmentalised by White feminists into separate boxes with no understanding of how they intersect. I have personally experienced my feminism and multiple representations being subjected to this level of ignorance and exclusion.

FEMINISM SO WHITE

This truth is self-evident that White women did not create historic or modern feminism. The face of feminism as predominantly White middle-class women has drawn strong criticism from different quarters. Primarily because it inevitably excludes a majority of Ethnic Minority feminists from mainstream feminist groups, organisations and platforms, because there isn't a sense of belonging. Even when Ethnic Minority women are at the forefront of feminism, they don't receive the same amount of coverage in the media or prominence, which does not help to create a sense of belonging or a diverse movement. The disparity is demonstrated in this cross-section of tweets:

Sharmaine Lovegrove #BlackLivesMatter @SharLovegrove
Jan 20 2019

> After the first #womensmarchlondon experiencing the wave of whiteness & lack of police (because nice white ladies protesting is not a threat but black people dancing at Notting Hill carnival is) I vowed never to go on this march again. If you're not intersectional I am not there.

Shaista Aziz @shaistaAziz Jan 20 2019

> #whitefeminism101:
> Yesterday @womensmarchlon young marchers were chanting about need to dismantle white supremacy and misogyny.
> An older white woman walked over and removed the megaphone from them saying: "this march is nothing to do with race." #whiteness is indeed toxic.

Shaista Aziz @shaistaAziz Jan 20 2019

> My friend, a brilliant Black South African woman walked
> over to the woman and told her to give the megaphone
> back telling her: "you do not get to silence us, not here, not
> anywhere."
> #WomensMarchLondon
> #weainthereforyou

J.K. Frederick @JayKFrederick Jan 22 2018

> Dear @SholaMos1 brilliant event yesterday – thank you!
> Diversity definitely represented from the stage but on the
> ground I must disagree numbers of black and brown women
> and men of all colours very low. Look at the images taken.
> Hope for improvement next march! @BBCWomansHour

Feminism is not a product or social construct of White women. Regardless of any contemporary research, theory or history you read, you will find that feminism has existed since the beginning of time. You will find women from different cultures and societies who were the first of many disrupters of the status quo, leaders in their own right and change makers. From continent to continent, history reveals women who have made both incremental and significant changes in their societies, some of which have been adopted by other societies. One thing these feminists will have in common is that they are disruptors, but the key difference between them is their personalities, class, race, culture and so on. It is because of the diversity of their multiple representation that their impact is widespread beyond their respective societies.

A century after certain women first won the right to vote, there are issues that remain significantly divisive in the feminist movement, including, but not limited to, political participation, Trans rights, abortion rights, race, class and sex-worker rights, to name a few. The truth is that the liberation of all women is interlinked and transcends the boundaries of race, class and sexuality. This does not mean women are one unified block on every issue, however I think it means that though we may share common goals, the paths we take to achieve them will differ, and it is the right of every woman to determine her own path. We can achieve this without erasing another's reality or prioritising one choice above others. Feminists can only succeed in breaking down the patriarchy if we do it consciously and undivided.

Yet Black women have been excluded and marginalised in feminist spaces predominantly led by White women to the detriment of causes that directly impact the quality of life and choice of Black women. Some White women place their reality/choices above that of Black women or place conditions on working on causes that are a priority for Black women. In reality, they pay lip service to Black rights by wilfully choosing not to dismantle one of the biggest threats to Black women – White supremacy. This is because their way of life is predicated on denying an equal value of life and liberty to Black people. Please note that I speak of 'some' not 'all' White women.

The same structural barriers of racism and prejudice are often demonstrated in some of these feminist spaces. Some White women's subconscious and innate desire to 'control' these spaces is the manifestation of White supremacy against Black women. This happens in the very feminist spaces where every woman should feel free from subjugation. It is important that White feminists undertake a deep dive into the historical context of White supremacy, and what their role was in benefiting from and reproducing it actively or passively, in order to ensure they recognise what actions they can take today to be better and effective allies to Black women. bell hooks sums this up thus:

'Consequently, it can be easily argued that even though white men institutionalized slavery, white women were its most immediate beneficiaries. Slavery in no way altered the hierarchical social status of the white male but it created a new status for the white female. The only way that her new status could be maintained was through the constant assertion of her superiority over the black woman and man. All too often colonial white women, particularly those who were slave mistresses, chose to differentiate their status from the slave's by treating the slave in a brutal and cruel manner. It was in her relationship to the black female slave that the white woman could best assert her power.'*

It is possible to be a White feminist and racist, and to be a White moderate and racist. The commonality is the exclusion and stereotyping of Black feminists in overt and covert ways in the feminist movement. It is a manifestation of the systemic oppression of White supremacy to weaponise their Whiteness, just as the colonial White women did to differentiate their status.

---

* bell hooks, *Ain't I a Woman: Black Women and Feminism,* South End Press, 1981.

INTERSECTIONAL FEMINISM

'There are many, many different kinds of intersectional exclusions – not just black women but other women of color. Not just people of color, but people with disabilities. Immigrants. LGBTQ people. Indigenous people.'*

American lawyer, civil rights advocate, philosopher, and a leading scholar of critical race theory, Kimberlé Williams Crenshaw

Is the feminist movement intersectional? I find we talk the talk of intersectionality but don't practise what we preach. Are we intersectional, Feminism *Oh So White?* How about Feminism *Not So Trans* or Feminism *Not So Muslim?* How about Feminism *Not For Sex Workers?* Intersectionality highlights the complexity of feminism. When you combine different equality categories, such as class, gender, race, faith, age, dis/ability, migrant background, ethnicity, sexual orientation or socio-economic background and others, it captures how the absence of intersectionality manifests inequality. There are aspects of the feminist movement today that do not in any way resemble feminism because of those within the movement who pay lip service to the objective of feminism but cause division when other women don't conform to their ideology of feminism.

These tweets demonstrate the challenge of intersectional feminism in the movement, from denial of its existence to shunning feminists for their choices:

---

* HuffPost US, 8 November 2017, https://www.huffingtonpost.co.uk/entry/kimberle-crenshaw-intersectional-feminism_n_598de38de4b090964296a34d.

Caroline @CoachCaroline Jun 28 2020

> There is no such thing as intersectional feminism. In fact
> that is a movement that centers male rights, so by definition
> it's not feminist. You can't take a word, give it a random
> prefix and change the meaning of it. A trans woman is not a
> woman, he is a trans identified man.

Robyndoolittle ✔ @robyndoolittle Feb 5 2014

> Getting emails from women angry I posed for the Flare
> photo. I can be a feminist & wear heels & red lips. I posed
> because I felt like it.

Kimberlé Williams Crenshaw first coined the term 'intersectionality' to give structural intersection to multiple forms of inequalities experienced by marginalised groups, particularly Black women, because treating these inequalities as mutually exclusive enforces discreet forms of oppression enabled by each inequality. Failure to recognise that multiple oppressions can be and are being experienced by a marginalised group enables a consistent destructive and toxic co-existence of inequality in people's lives. She further explains that 'Black women's intersectional experiences of racism and sexism have been a central but forgotten dynamic in the unfolding of feminist and antiracist agendas.'* Inequality is often perceived as centred on two distinct disadvantages, i.e. distribution of resources vs devaluation of identity. It premises that one can be economically deprived without being socially despised, as you can face social discrimination

---

* Kimberlé Williams Crenshaw, 'Black Women Still in Defense of Ourselves', from *Ain't Gonna Let Nobody Turn Me Around: Forty Years of Movement Building with Barbara Smith*, edited by Alethia Jones et al, p. 90.

without being economically deprived. This isn't true for marginalised groups. Gender as an example cuts across both the economic and social strata, so women can be economically/financially subordinate to men and also face social discrimination, particularly women from Ethnic Minorities. It is no longer enough to have equality laws highlighting conflicts between different equality categories. What we need is a real-time impact bridge that addresses the cumulative and combined reality of multiple inequalities. This can be critically achieved through intersectionality.

THE AFRO-VISIBLE FEMINIST

'All the myths and stereotypes used to characterize black womanhood have their roots in negative anti-woman mythology. Yet they form the basis of most critical inquiry into the nature of black female experience. Many people have difficulty appreciating black women as we are because of eagerness to impose an identity upon us based on any number of negative stereotypes.'*

bell hooks

I am going to draw from some of my experiences here. I think it is important to do so to give context to the challenges and barriers Black feminists face with being visible when their Black identity is stereotyped. I was one of the lead organisers of a women's rights movement and not for the first time in my life, the only Black woman. It is not important to me to name the organisation because that is not the point of sharing this. I am simply sharing my experience and lessons learnt. Suffice to say, it is also not about naming

---

* bell hooks, *Ain't I a Woman: Black Women and Feminism*, South End Press, 1981.

or shaming those who shaped my experiences there. For ease of reference, I will refer to it as the 'organisation'.

This organisation had been initially orchestrated and organised by White women. When I joined the organisation, I recall getting friendly advice from Black women that I should be careful not to be appropriated by this group and advised that spaces like this don't really represent Black women. Call me naïve, but I took their advice with a pinch of salt. I knew they meant well, but I think what I had seen of the women in the group did not suggest to me that I should be on my guard 24/7. To be honest with you, I was also very busy juggling multiple commitments and this group was only one aspect of many activities I was engaged with in my activism. However, the friendly advice was to come back to haunt me. I couldn't believe how long it took me to see what was right before my eyes with this group. I should certainly have known better. Two of the lessons I have since learned is that within all of the supposed feminist unity exist the stereotypes that plague the Black identity and that not all feminists are intersectional. The organisation ended up becoming, for me, a place of condemnation and judgement. It was a betrayal of everything I knew feminism to be and an attack on my Afro-Visible Feminism.

I became one of the vocal voices and visible faces of the group because I was asked to do so by the pre-existing organisers, who were two White women. I spoke my own words and thoughts when called to represent the organisation but I did so on the understanding it was all in solidarity. So, I was quite surprised when it started to dawn on me that this had become a problem for the two White women, who started to complain that I was too loud, dominant and visible. I recall a dinner that they had invited me to just before I was to speak at a prestigious event. The central message I took away from the dinner conversation with both women was to inform me that they had created the organisation to give everyone a space, particularly Black women like me, and that it is important for people to know that the organisation is not led by one woman. This became a constant theme, as though it was necessary for me to be reminded – I didn't think much more of it at the time, as I thought it was their way of conveying their thoughts and that some people feel comfortable doing it on repeat. In hindsight, I was very naïve not to see that I was being perceived as a threat to what they had worked for and that they were not happy at how visible I had become. More crucially is that, as time went on, I realised it was not just being visible that was the problem but that, in their words, I was too dominant and could not be contained.

I recall a picture of me shaking hands with Theresa May at the Windrush event in 2018 at No. 10 Downing Street being the subject of contention at the organisation, even though my presence at the event was unconnected to it. Literally every organiser (except one) called me to take it down from my social media pages because being seen shaking hands with Theresa May would be toxic for 'everything the organisation has worked for'. This was the phrase used by one of the two White lead co-organisers. My picture with Theresa May was equated to the fallout of Theresa May holding hands with Donald Trump in 2017 at the White House. There was nothing truthful or rational about this position. I was genuinely stunned by the double standard, especially given the organisation had no qualms publicly with being associated with a charity that had just undergone an international sexual abuse scandal, the association of which could potentially cause reputational risk to the organisation. They were more concerned about how *my* picture with Theresa May would cause irrevocable damage and claimed it was a timing issue with a campaign we were organising at the time. I understood in that moment how necessary and multifaceted my representation is. I could see that they did not understand that, as a Black woman, I am more than one thing to multiple causes and my feminism cannot be controlled or manipulated to fit one narrative. I am a Black woman who represents multiple struggles. I don't get to choose which struggle I represent on any given day, neither does one struggle trump another. I am one and all, similar to many women of colour. For some, that picture represented a whole lot more than Theresa May shaking Shola's hand.

I took the time to articulate my views on the double standards and saw it as a learning opportunity to educate my fellow co-organisers on what and who I represent. The principle of the matter is that Windrush was another clear discrimination against Black people in the UK. Many fought to hold the government accountable and, even more so, make Windrush a national day of celebration on its 70th anniversary. I was very critical of Theresa May's government's decisions during her time as Prime Minister and Home Secretary – from the 'hostile environment', Windrush, Grenfell to Brexit and more. Many other prominent Black personalities who also criticised the government attended that reception and many of us shook Theresa May's hand. It was also courteous to do so. Criticising her does not mean I can't shake her hand and I should not have to justify it to anyone. I raised the question of how the organisation could claim to be a platform for many voices but see a picture of its Black organiser with the Prime Minister at a Windrush event as a reputational risk? What about the Black voices and Windrush? Are these not voices to be supported? I wear multiple hats and was not at Downing Street because of the organisation. How could shaking hands with Theresa May at a Windrush celebration be more destructive to the organisation's reputation than its association with a charity facing a backlash for an international sexual abuse scandal? Though I agreed to take down the image on my Twitter account (but not other social media accounts) for the duration of the campaign the organisation was organising at the time, I was clear that next time I didn't agree with something I wouldn't do it unless I found the rationale persuasive and sound. The perceived risk of these two White women was a direct attempt to silence my representation. If I had not changed the narrative on this, positioned my multifaceted representation and feminism clearly, my voice would have been lost and my identity as a Black woman compromised and forced into a box.

Shortly after this, the organisation became really toxic and I was blamed for that toxicity. At some point the two White women left the group, leaving me, three women of colour activists (not Black) and another White activist as the core group. It took an external culture review of the organisation for me to finally understand what was going on. In the vacuum of the two White women leaving, apparently there was 'fear' that I would dominate and lead. For the record, I had no interest in doing so and as far as I was aware there was no hierarchy within the group, so this was a surprise to me. My style, by those in the group, was referred to as 'atypical' and needing 'moderation' and 'containment' so as not to dominate. Every description used of me fitted the stereotype of the 'angry Black woman': dominant, a bully, threatening, can't be contained, etc. Furthermore, it was clear to me that having a difference of opinion became the root cause for my character assassination. I just did not understand why. But this summation by the external reviewer is what finally opened my eyes as to the 'why'. I am referred to by the initials SMS:

'It is also important to note the ways in which SMS was atypical of the existing make-up of ▓▓ [the organisation]: SMS brought with her new skills, personality, expertise, style and is a highly educated professional, legally trained black African woman. A distinct intersectional presence, SMS is also an articulate, bold individual with an unmistakable style who expresses herself confidently on a number of issues, including legal ones, and refuses to be "contained" by others' expectations. She is also the only black (African descent) woman in the core organising and coordinating functions of ■■ [the organisation], which itself is part of a wider movement (the feminist movement) which has historically been dominated by white middle class women from the global north – a weakness which feminists have for decades grappled with. She is of course one of many women of colour in the organisation. However, the distinctive combination of her intersectional location, combined with her personal qualities and conduct, seems to have posed a challenge to ■■ [the organisation] which it has, as yet, not been able to rise to.'

The penny dropped – this was a light bulb moment, because finally I understood that everything that I am and represent was problematic for this group. The very intersectionality I represented was too loud, visible and dominant, so it was unwelcome. I was unwelcome in a space that should represent all women, including me. Particularly because I could not be 'contained', or what they really meant: controlled. Any accomplishment I had was atypical and seen as a threat. The presence and actions of other women of colour only served to legitimise and reinforce the racial ignorance, stereotyping and intolerance I was experiencing in the group. It was a toxic, polarising and isolating experience that went against everything I believed feminism to be. I am a very private person, so sharing this is a departure from the norm. It is the first time I am doing so because I believe it is important. As a woman of faith, I take every issue to God and trust in Him to see me through, which He did. I definitely don't want another Black woman to experience this and hope my shared experiences will help other White, Black, Asian and Ethnic Minority intersectional feminists to, in the words of Audre Lorde, recognise, accept and celebrate differences.

FEMINISM *NOT SO TRANS*

The exclusion of Trans women by some in the feminist movement is deeply disturbing. I don't pretend to be well versed in the nuances of the layered debates between Trans women fighting for their right to be recognised as women and biologically born women who feel threatened that the rights of Trans women may erase their biological rights as women. But I find it very disturbing at how unfeminist and non-intersectional this is. I think any decent human being would agree that exclusion, rejection and ostracising is unacceptable. These behaviours replicate the experiences women have had with the patriarchy and so it genuinely beggars belief that we would replicate these behaviours within a movement that should be inclusive and intersectional. Even more so for Black Trans women, who are dealing with multiple intersecting inequalities, which puts them at a significant risk of discrimination and violence. We cannot, as women and feminists, contribute to or have a vested interest in the exploitation and dehumanisation of other women. I will tell you why this is my business. I think it is my business to support my fellow women who are Trans women to ensure their equal rights and freedom because their liberation is linked to mine. I don't think it is my business to determine their informed and considered choices. Social media, as always, reflects the ongoing discussions around Trans rights as demonstrated by these tweets:

J.K. Rowling ✔ @jk_rowling Jun 6 2020

If sex isn't real, there's no same-sex attraction. If sex isn't real, the lived reality of women globally is erased. I know and love trans people, but erasing the concept of sex removes the ability of many to meaningfully discuss their lives. It isn't hate to speak the truth.

Homunculus @tryingattimes Jun 22 2020

'Woman' is already inclusive.

It is inclusive of all races, all ages past adolescence, all physical abilities or disabilities, all personalities, all sexual orientations, all politics, all sartorial preferences, throughout the ages.

That's all, and that's all it needs to be.

Protect Trans Kids / BLM ✔ @MunroeBergdorf Jul 5 2020

If you want to know what is best for trans people. Listen to trans people.

More specifically, listen to black trans women who are navigating covid19, racism & transphobia.

Listen to supportive parents of trans kids who have watched their kids flourish after being listened to.

Julia Hartley-Brewer ✔ @JuliaHB1 Jun 28 2020

Replying to @StephenKing

Do you have a daughter? Are you happy for a man who claims to be a woman to be naked in a changing room with her? Really?

There is undoubtedly a need for a calm exchange of information to address the concerns and fears between the dissenting and concurring voices in order to reach a place of understanding and common purpose. In my opinion, Sex is real and Trans is real. 'Woman' is enough to include all women (Biological and Trans) without erasing either of our realities. The intersectionality of Trans women is largely ignored or denied by feminists whose fear of Trans women is rooted in an erasure of the biologically born female identity. I do not agree with this. Trans women are no threat to me as a biologically born woman or threat to my rights as a woman. Our human and women's rights are interlinked and the same in many respects. By acting on their fear against Trans women, these feminists are manifesting and amplifying existing inequalities on an already marginalised group. I am speaking specifically about feminists whose abuse of Trans women is to segregate them from the sisterhood of women. Feminism is about integration not segregation. A Black Trans woman can experience multiple intersecting discriminations and prejudices in a non-intersectional feminist movement. Trans women being treated unequally is the antithesis of the equality the women's rights and feminist movement fight for. Intersectionality of Black Trans women also appears to trigger the White supremacy of some White feminists.

While doing the dishes at home with my fourteen-year-old daughter, we had a conversation about the ongoing war between TERFs and Trans activists. Particularly about how Trans women are treated in the feminist movement and the impact on Black Trans women. She admits she is still researching the issues but feels strongly about the protection of Trans rights. Her passion for and knowledge of the issues was enlightening. Here's a snapshot of our dialogue – for ease of reference I will refer to my daughter and I by the first letter of our names.

S: *In my view, sex is real and Trans is real. Being Trans does not negate that sex is real. Is that too simplistic?*

O: No, it is not. No Trans women I'm aware of have said sex isn't real. They've said 'I am a woman' and 'I want to live my life as a woman'. That is who they are and identify as.

S: *Why do you think the issue has become problematic among feminists?*

O: The problem is victimizing the TERF community while advancing transphopia against the Trans community. The TERF community tend to put on the mask of feminism but the main goal is stripping all Trans people of rights. Even though Trans women should have the same rights as Cis women.

S: *What is a TERF?*

O: A radical feminist who excludes Trans women: Trans-exclusionary Radical Feminist.

S: *Okay and what is Cis?*

O: Biologically born woman whose gender identity matches her biological sex.

S: *What do you think of J. K. Rowling's comments about Trans people?*

O: The issues are much bigger than J. K. Rowling. I don't think she is doing it on purpose to hurt people. I just think she's misinformed. I felt her response to the transphobic allegations against her[*] was helpful to give an understanding of her views, but it was misinformed in some parts, which can put Trans rights and lives in danger. Her support of Maya Forstater and Magdalen Berns was no longer just about 'sex

---

[*] J. K. Rowling's response to transphobic allegations, https://www.jkrowling.com/opinions/j-k-rowling-writes-about-her-reasons-for-speaking-out-on-sex-and-gender-issues/.

is real' because of the things they were saying about the Trans community. She also raised concerns about letting Trans women use women's restrooms as a danger to women, even though she acknowledged Trans women are subjected to abuse as well. This stoked up phobia against Trans women.

S: *Do you think there is any truth to this phobia about the restrooms?*

O: No, Mummy. There have never been mass cases of Trans women sexually attacking Cis women. When I researched it, those who had were paedophiles! And I doubt that Trans women would go through body changes, gender identity, therapy, pills just so they can look at women in the bathroom! Imagine if Trans women were forced to go to the men's restroom, there would be a far higher chance of them being abused and their lives in danger than Trans women using Cis women's restroom. This is willingly prioritising the safety of Cis women over Trans women and that is not okay.

S: *How do you think this affects Black Trans women?*

O: Black people have a lot to deal with and just by the colour of their skin suffer a systemic disadvantage plus the disadvantages suffered by Trans people. Black Trans women are more likely to be in danger and less advantaged than White Trans women.

S: *I hear you but there are feminists who aren't TERFs who think there are legitimate concerns around the erasure of sex.*

O: But these don't have to be two different things! There's no reason why feminism and Trans rights have to be two different things. Trans women are women and feminists too! Don't turn them away. I am not saying Trans women are exactly like Cis women, they have different experiences. A

Black Cis woman has a different experience from a White Cis woman but they are both still women!

S: *What do you think should happen next in this whole discourse on Trans rights?*

O: I think Trans women should be treated equally as women and Trans men equally as men. Trans women should not be denied access to women's restrooms because who they are doesn't necessarily match what is in between their legs. TERF women's narrow-minded view of femininity doesn't just affect Trans women but non-binary people too. Trans rights pose no threat to women whatsoever and there is no danger in everybody being treated equally. We have to stop putting up false risks and false dangers. We have to see people as people. Talk to them, understand them and see who they are. Then you will be surprised that they are not worried or confused about their identities. We need to drop our preconceived ideas of gender identity and actually talk to Trans people. We can then fight together as one feminist movement and then things can really change. We need to stand and fight together.

FEMINISM *NOT SO MALE*

I'm proud to say my Afro-Visible Feminism includes men. This might be an unpopular position among more conservative feminists, but that's okay. While we fight the patriarchal structural inequality, we must remember that men can be our allies in our resistance. Men are our brothers, husbands, sons, friends and colleagues, so including them is part of the solution not the problem. My father, Prince Adebajo Babington-Ashaye, was the first male feminist in my life. He believed in me and taught me I could be anything I wanted to be. There was never a sense with him that there were limitations and barriers to who I can be as a woman. I know I am extremely lucky to have had such a father. I remember him telling me when I was fourteen years old that the best legacy he could leave my siblings and I was our education. Which is why he worked hard and aspired for us to go to the best schools. He once told me that even if parents leave kids with property and money when they died, these were material things that could be taken from the children, but nobody can take from them a good education. He was so right. Today I pass on the values of a good and strong education to my own three children.

As far as I am concerned, the term feminist is gender neutral. Any gender can be a feminist. Earlier in this chapter, I explained what feminism is to me. It is about women, yes, but the advocacy for women's rights is not limited to, and should not be restricted to, women alone. That is a very lonely prospect. Representation is a powerful thing and if we want to change the behaviour of men steeped in patriarchy and end the objectification of women, then male advocates of women's rights must be allowed to be effective models of representation to other men by wearing their feminism as badges of honour. They should be allowed to be at the forefront and not just the background of the feminist movement. Now there will be some who will vehemently disagree with me on allowing men anywhere near the front and claim that's taking spaces belonging to women. I respectfully disagree. I'm talking about ending the bickering among some feminists who don't even want men in the vicinity of the women's rights movement and can only tolerate them being in the shadows. Fighting sexism and misogyny requires a united effort because the incessant casual sexism and misogyny experienced by women needs to be resisted by men too, as allies. Advocating for an equal playing field so that opportunities and outcomes apply to women equally is something lesser men must see better men do. This is only one of many reasons for including men in the feminist movement. In a brilliant essay written by former US President Barack Obama, he encourages men to fight against gender stereotypes and double standards. He was the first US President in office to openly proclaim he is a feminist. In his words, 'It is absolutely men's responsibility to fight sexism too. And as spouses and partners and boyfriends, we need to work hard and be deliberate about creating truly equal relationships.'* I could not agree with Obama more. Men should wear feminism with pride and help fight against gender discrimination and stereotypes designed to belittle women and limit our progress.

CONCLUDING THOUGHTS . . .

'It is obvious that many women have appropriated feminism to serve their own ends, especially those white women who have been at the forefront of the movement; but rather than resigning myself to this appropriation I choose to re-appropriate the term "feminism," to focus on the fact that to be "feminist" in any authentic sense of the term is to want for all people, female and male, liberation from sexist role patterns, domination, and oppression.'†

bell hooks

Feminism should not just be a declaration but a demonstration. It should not be a claim to a title but a manifestation of who you are.

---

* 'Glamour Exclusive: President Barack Obama Says, "This Is What A Feminist Looks Like"', *Glamour*, 4 August 2016, https://www.glamour.com/story/glamour-exclusive-president-barack-obama-says-this-is-what-a-feminist-looks-like.
† bell hooks, *Ain't I a Woman?: Black Women and Feminism*, South End Press, 1981.

The equality that feminism seeks should not just be about equal opportunities and outcomes in comparison to men. Equality should also be about freedom from the judgement, prejudice and oppressive pressures from within the feminist movement. It should be about safe spaces for all feminists to grow, make mistakes, learn and progress. We are human, so mistakes are inevitable and so is growth. We will sometimes take the wrong turn. A true application of intersectionality as a mode of conduct in our daily lives as we interact and intersect will show many of us 'learning to walk' as if we were babies. That is okay. What is not okay is deliberate and continued ignorance or refusal to learn.

True feminism manifests itself in our choices and lifestyles. It is our responsibility to respect our different brands of feminism. Whether a woman is a stripper or sex worker, it does not make her less feminist. Professions don't define feminism. We create a mess in the feminist movement by bringing our personal bias and prejudice to play as though we don't have enough of a fight on our hands with the patriarchy. We need to check our privilege and bias to understand how it impacts our relationships with other feminists, which inevitably impacts the feminist movement. Drops of water make a mighty ocean. We are all the many parts of one body and should work together.

Feminism recognises and celebrates the individual woman as well as the collective power of many women. It strengthens the individual power of a single woman while, at the same time, taking the different strengths each woman represents into one powerful collective voice. All for one and one for all. This is what feminism is to me. It doesn't seek to change who I am or make me conform. Feminists come in different shapes of opinions, passion, politics and causes. We have different life experiences that shape what our feminism is, which means feminism itself is subjective. It means feminists should be recognised, in the first instance, as individuals rather than just contributors or victims of a cause. Give each woman room to express their own brand of feminism, which has been shaped by their life experiences and choices. Feminists have different personalities and are different people. We are not meant to be the same. It is quite puzzling to me that there are feminists within the movement who don't get this logic. One's feminism can be an effective bridge to neutralise division and embrace differences. We are all women with one goal in sight – to fulfil our dreams and goals, whatever they may be. However, our journey to achieving this may differ because we have different experiences and make different choices. Feminists are not meant to sound and look the same or make the same choices as another feminist. Feminism isn't a cult. Some of us are quiet, loud, strong minded, opinionated, softly spoken but firm, doers, talkers, etc.

Only bold and ambitious women make history. Humility is a virtue worth having but not a substitute for boldness. Humility is not the evidence or lack thereof of confidence. There is no shame in being an ambitious woman. If being well-behaved and humble means I have to wait a turn, know my place or ask permission, then I don't want to be well-behaved. It is certainly not my understanding of humility. The fact that you are humble does not mean you can't be confident or boldly resist the obstacles in your way or fight the injustice and inequality you experience and witness. *This is why I resist.*

I am without a doubt unapologetically ambitious, unashamedly bold and unequivocally vocal. Feminism should be an authentic representation of a woman's true nature, growth and experience at every point of her life. A representation of her freedom of choice and independence. If you have a problem with my Afro-Visible Feminism, then you have a problem with me. If being ambitious, bold and vocal offends your sensibilities, then please be offended, because feminism is not a one-trick pony. Don't try to define my feminism because my feminism can only be a true reflection of me.

Bold women find courage where there seems to be no courage, resilient in the face of immense adversity and able to step outside their comfort zone to do something different. They say no to power, say yes when circumstances dictate otherwise and refuse to conform.

We must let feminism breathe – it should be flexible, adaptable and fluid, because that is what we are as human beings. To do less will create a static, rigid and inflexible feminism that will fail women at their most vulnerable. My brand of feminism represents me and if we accept that feminism is first the individual, then feminism is multifaceted, multi-representational and fluid. If you identify as a feminist, someone who wants equality for women, freedom of choice for all, etc., then you must accept that equality and freedom of choice means the ability to make good or poor choices and take different paths, and that there is fluidity in the choices we make that are shaped by our life experiences.

I am genuinely fortunate to know some awesome White feminists whom I count as friends, sisters and allies. These women, along with my Black, Asian and Ethnic Minority feminist friends, are wholesome women who genuinely manifest solidarity, empathy and strength. However, solidarity and empathy require the kind of strength that visibly stands up to racism and eradicates the dehumanisation of Black women.

This is why I resist.

7

WHO'S PLAYING IDENTITY POLITICS?

'In this country American means white. Everybody else
has to hyphenate.' *

Nobel Laureate, Toni Morrison

The biggest identity played in politics is the White identity, used to
discredit, discount and delegitimise marginalised groups in order to
make way for one dominant group. Marginalised groups are based on
a shared identity with distinct struggles that co-exist but are ultimately sidelined by one dominant identity. It is undeniable that the
dominant identity in British and American politics is White identity
politics. This is the politics that centres Whiteness as the standard,
code and priority for governing and navigating societal affairs. It predominantly sees White, Male, Straight, Able-bodied and Christian
faith as the default. It enforces and enables White supremacy as the
rule of thumb in government both internationally and nationally.
White identity politics is the agitated response of White people in
Britain and America to increasing racial diversity in both countries.

Politics has become a cesspool and a reflection of the polarised
society we live in. What should be a multi-faceted means of representation that gives equal voice to the experiences and needs of

---

* Toni Morrison, *Guardian*, 29 January 1992.

different identities is the exact opposite. Politics today ignores the need to recognise how marginalised identities intersect for a fairer and more equitable society. White identity politics is the weaponisation of Whiteness in Britain and America that is populist, culturally and racially motivated. American journalist Ezra Klein explores the impact of a dominant identity on other groups:

> 'The term "identity politics", in this usage, obscures rather than illuminates; it's used to diminish and discredit the concerns of the weaker groups by making them look self-interested, special pleading in order to clear the agenda for the concerns of stronger groups, which are framed as more rational, proper topics for political debate.'*

I agree with this summation. White identity politics does not promote a positive White racial identity. This is evidenced by the recent political climate in both America and Britain. It seeks to diminish other shared identities for the sole objective of enforcing White supremacy. In the words of John F. Kennedy, 'the rights of every man are diminished when the rights of one man are threatened.' This perspective is clearly lost on the propagators of White identity politics who see racial diversity as a threat and expound their irrational fear that they will no longer be a dominant voice with political, social and economic dominance. There is clearly an inherent irrational and unfounded fear of their Whiteness being erased by making way for racial diversity. These mindsets, fuelled by a hunger for White identity politics, are the same mindset that created and enforced slavery, colonialism, segregation and continual denial of an equal value of life and liberty to Black people. How? The dominance sought by White

---

* Ezra Klein, *Why We're Polarized*, Avid Reader Press, 2020.

identity politics is a return to a time Britain and America were White nations with exclusive political, social and economic dominance built on the backs, blood, sweat and deaths of Black people in and out of Africa.

White identity politics is the face of the shameful state of politics today, where the voices of marginalised identities are not given equal representation in the corridors of power; the powerful speak through elite politicians, and politicians are allowed to get away with lies, extraordinary admissions of impropriety, spreading and defending misinformation, as well as abuse of office. Policies, spending cuts and decision-making that impact our daily lives are made without real accountability and with a different set of standards than those that apply to the rest of us. There is no threshold of misinformation and shame for politicians.

This has led to a profound depth of public distrust in politics, politicians and the electoral process. Any form of real trust is completely eroded today. As an example, no current political party leaders or head of state in America or Britain command the complete confidence and trust of the electorate. From Brexit and Trump to Boris Johnson, we exist in a politics of rhetoric, division and no accountability. It is a vicious cycle of belittling the public's intelligence, widening the public's distrust of politicians and constructively denying the public access to *all* information that will enable the electorate to make informed decisions. The media is complicit in this. There is no doubt that since the Brexit referendum in June 2016 and Trump's inauguration in January 2017, politics has become an extremely volatile tribal state of affairs rooted in White supremacy. The politics of White supremacy is White identity politics.

Politics has disintegrated into personal attacks not just against and between politicians but by politicians against non-politicians they do not agree with. It shows a mean-spiritedness unworthy of our society and public office. Disagreement, debate and difference of opinion is healthy and perfectly fine, but not hate-filled rhetoric and deliberate mischaracterisation. Politicians should first serve the country before their political party. But recent years have shown that many politicians deny their conscience by putting personal ambitions and party politics above the country they were placed in power to serve and protect. This is a clear departure from the wise words of former US President Harry Truman when he said 'let us keep our eyes on the issues and work for the things we all believe in. Let each of us put our country ahead of our party, and ahead of our own personal interests'.* It is also a departure from Winston Churchill, who said:

> 'The first duty of a member of Parliament is to do what he thinks in his faithful and disinterested judgement is right and necessary for the honour and safety of Great Britain. His second duty is to his constituents, of whom he is the representative but not the delegate. Burke's famous declaration on this subject is well known. It is only in the third place that his duty to party organization or programme takes rank. All these three loyalties should be observed, but there is no doubt of the order in which they stand under any healthy manifestation of democracy.'†

While I am a strong critic of Churchill, whose racist beliefs and views were steeped in White supremacy that dehumanises the Black identity, he and Truman are correct that politics should be centred on what's best for the whole country first above party and

---

* Harry S. Truman, State of the Union Address, 8 January 1951.
† Winston Churchill, 'Duties of a Member of Parliament', *c.* 1954–1955.

self-preservation. This has definitely not been the case in the era of Brexit and Trumpism.

THE POLITICS OF DIVISION

White identity politics has normalised divisive rhetoric in present-day politics, particularly in how it impacts the lives of Black people. This divisiveness is rooted in race, immigration, gender, religion and far-right populism. It is exemplified by mass shootings executed by Trump supporters, the murder of a UK MP over Brexit, and the premiership of Boris Johnson running on the fumes of the right-wing populism of Brexit. We watch in bewilderment as opposing views rise to defend the indefensible, attempting to deflect from the catastrophic consequences of the division utilised by Donald Trump and Boris Johnson. The oppressiveness of this language of division dehumanises the Black identity and is aptly described by Toni Morrison as violent:

'Oppressive language does more than represent violence; it is violence; does more than represent the limits of knowledge; it limits knowledge. Whether it is obscuring state language or the faux-language of mindless media; whether it is the proud but calcified language of the academy or the commodity driven language of science; whether it is the malign language of law-without-ethics, or language designed for the estrangement of minorities, hiding its racist plunder in its literary cheek – it must be rejected, altered and exposed. It is the language that drinks blood, laps vulnerabilities, tucks its fascist boots under crin-olines of respectability and patriotism as it moves relentlessly toward the bottom line and the bottomed-out mind. Sexist language, racist language, theistic language – all are typical of the policing languages of mastery, and cannot, do not permit new knowledge or encourage the mutual exchange of ideas.'*

It is not just that the violence of intolerance, lies and misinformation promote divisions that are rife in politics, it is the fact that the perpetrators of this terrible behaviour are allowed to get away with it. Journalist Peter Oborne has shed light on the complicity of the media in fostering this behaviour. In his *Guardian* piece on Boris Johnson, he asserted the reason for mainstream media turning a blind eye:

'A big reason for Johnson's easy ride is partisanship from the parts of the media determined to get him elected. I have talked to senior BBC executives, and they tell me they personally think it's wrong to expose lies told by a British prime minister because it undermines trust in British politics. Is that a reason for giving Johnson free rein to make any false claim he wants?'†

It is beyond outrageous for anyone to consider it reasonable that calling out a Prime Minister as a liar is seen as more destructive to UK democracy than the actual lies of the Prime Minister or the decisions of the public predicated on those lies. This is aiding and abetting on an industrial scale and should *not* be what politics should look like. But the media is another institution in which Whiteness is centred, to the detriment of all other identities.

---

* Toni Morrison, Nobel Lecture, 1993.
† Peter Obourne, 'It's not just Boris Johnson's lying. It's that the media let him get away with it', *Guardian*, 18 November 2019, https://www.theguardian.com/commentisfree/2019/nov/18/boris-johnson-lying-media.

Donald Trump, notorious for his offensive tweets, did not suffer any consequences for his deeply racist, misogynist and xenophobic tweets against Congresswomen Ocasio-Cortez of New York, Rashida Tlaib of Michigan, Ilhan Omar of Minnesota and Ayanna Pressley of Massachusetts. The barrage of defences put up to protect an overtly racist US President was staggering. It was clear that politics, politicians and polarised American society had become morally bankrupt, but even worse are civilians who defend this behaviour because it reflects their own thinking and beliefs. I have debated the issue of Trump's racist tweets several times, among other disturbing escalating behaviour of his presidency, on live television, and I am no longer surprised at the outstanding sheer audacity of those who vehemently defend Trump's rights to be racist, xenophobic and a misogynist. Trump exemplifies the violence of sexist, racist and misogynist language that is the mastery of White identity politics. The violent impact is visible to the eye: increased online abuse that emboldens more racism, sexism and misogyny against these four women whose shared identities come from marginalised groups which are being threatened and silenced by the onslaught of weaponising Whiteness in politics. These four Congresswomen represented everything White identity politics fears – the racial diversity of America. Social media was awash with differing views in response to Trump like these tweets:

Donald J. Trump ✔ @realDonaldTrump Jul 14 2019

So interesting to see "Progressive" Democrat Congresswomen, who originally came from countries whose governments are a complete and total catastrophe, the worst, most corrupt and inept anywhere in the world (if they even have a functioning government at all), now loudly......

Donald J. Trump ✔ @realDonaldTrump Jul 14 2019

… and viciously telling the people of the United States, the greatest and most powerful Nation on earth, how our government is to be run. Why don't they go back and help fix the totally broken and crime infested places from which they came. Then come back and show us how. …

Donald J. Trump ✔ @realDonaldTrump Jul 14 2019

… it is done. These places need your help badly, you can't leave fast enough. I'm sure that Nancy Pelosi would be very happy to quickly work out free travel arrangements!

Martha McC_ART @martha_mccart Jul 15 2019

Replying to **@realDonaldTrump**

These young liberal congresswomen are clueless to what America is about. It's truly about defending legal immigrants and those born here who support the American dream. I'm 100% Lebanese with Lebanese immigrant grandparents. Get out of Congress or protect Americans first!

Depth Quester @DepthQuester Jul 17 2019

Every other thing he says is twisted into racism. The **tweet** about **progressives** was a criticism of their politics coming from a nationalistic POV & liberals opted to see it as **racist** instead. Liberals have told me to leave the country for the same reasons **Trump** did.

Not evidence.

Palmer Report ✔ @PalmerReport Jul 14 2019

> Hey Donald Trump, you seem confused as to why these four non-white women in Congress are trying to tell the people "how our government is to be run." It's because they were elected to do exactly that, you fucking dumbass. #RacistInChief

THE IDENTITY POLITICS OF THE BREXIT ERA AND TRUMPISM

'The worst illiterate is the political illiterate, he doesn't hear, doesn't speak, nor participates in the political events. He doesn't know the cost of life, the price of the bean, of the fish, of the flour, of the rent, of the shoes and of the medicine, all depends on political decisions. The political illiterate is so stupid that he is proud and swells his chest saying that he hates politics. The imbecile doesn't know that, from his political ignorance is born the prostitute, the abandoned child, and the worst thieves of all, the bad politician, corrupted and flunky of the national and multinational companies.' *

Bertolt Brecht

Playwright Bertolt Brecht's quote on the political illiterate aptly describes my assessment of a section of the populace that voted for Brexit, and put Donald Trump and Boris Johnson in power. Brecht's view of political illiteracy does not suggest that they lack

---

* Quoted in Shehla Burney, *Representation and Reception: Brechtian 'Pedagogics of Theatre' and Critical Thinking*, Peter Lang, 2018.

education, so they are not illiterate in the academic sense. I think he speaks to the ambivalence, wilful ignorance and complacency some voters have towards politics, which forms the basis of their political illiteracy and ignorance. References to lack of knowledge on prices of beans, medicine, shoes and rent relates to how the politically illiterate live in a vacuum of inactive participation in politics. They don't connect the dots of the economics of the cost of living to the power of politics in governing everything from the food we eat and the clothes on our backs to the roof over our heads. He is saying that the inactive and politically illiterate cause more harm than good because the result of their political illiteracy and ignorance is to create a society that is politically ill-informed and inactive, which is, inevitably, a cancer to a healthy democracy. The politically illiterate say they hate politics but yet find in politics the means to express outrage at the discontent in their lives. This is the backdrop to White identity politics.

White identity politics birthed Trumpism and Brexit, which are centred on White nationalism and the control of immigration to assuage the grievance and fear that the ethnocultural identity of White people is being erased and/or dominated by racial diversity. What's worse is that this reveals the state of high political illiteracy in America and Britain, particularly with how it has been weaponised to feed the most primal fears of some White people. This political illiteracy undoubtedly transcends class, wealth, age, gender, faith, education, ethnicity, sexual orientation and political party. This is because it is centred on irrational hostility against non-White people, racial diversity and the multiculturalism they represent. What is clear is that those White people who buy into this messaging and follow a propaganda of White identity politics are ready to believe lies, conspiracies, share misinformation and manifest the violence of oppressive language they are sold. Regardless of who they are, from high-profile names to working-class White people, the common thread that binds them is weaponising Whiteness in the discourse and representation of politics. The White politically illiterate in America and Britain are under an illusion of fighting for sovereignty (Britain) or freedom (America), when in truth neither was ever lost. The irrefutable fact is that, within White identity politics, the politically illiterate are on a leash led by the White politically literate, who understand the economics of politics, actively participate in politics and push a divisive agenda for self-promotion, the consequences of which will be borne by the White politically illiterate but mostly by marginalised non-White identities, particularly Black people.

Both Trumpism and Brexit are rooted in White supremacy, which dehumanises the Black identity, and both subscribe to a religion of hate. If religion is the belief in, and worship of, a controlling power, then I posit that racism, Islamophobia, antisemitism, homophobia and xenophobia are the controlled power of religion that White identity politics subscribes to. Not all White people subscribe to this, and many condemn these expressions of hate, but unfortunately they are the lone voices in an America and Britain where these expressions of hate are institutionally entrenched. Individually, each hate is as old as time, but the combined pursuit to suppress and oppress the shared injustices of non-White identities to subjugation can only be described as a religion of hate. It definitely got its blueprint from the injustices meted out during slavery and colonialism. This religion of hate has become a decisive tool in enforcing the disintegration of racial diversity, the violence of oppressive language and weaponising political illiteracy to silence injustices against non-White identities. This is not my politics. *This is why I resist.*

When Trump, in July 2020, announced that low-income housing will be prohibited from suburban America, he did not put forward a cogent rationale for depriving this much-needed basic housing right from the disadvantaged. Instead he overtly appealed to White people by tweeting this:

Donald J. Trump ✓ @realDonaldTrump Jul 29 2020

I am happy to inform all of the people living their Suburban Lifestyle Dream that you will no longer be bothered or financially hurt by having low income housing built in your neighborhood.

Donald J. Trump ✓ @realDonaldTrump Jul 29 2020

. . . Your housing prices will go up based on the market, and crime will go down. I have rescinded the Obama-Biden AFFH Rule.

Trump basically overturned a rule that was created to address historic patterns of segregation, stop house discrimination and increase fair housing choices so that inclusive communities will become the norm. Who would benefit or suffer from his decision? The people Trump seeks to disempower with this decision are low-income residents, predominantly African Americans who disproportionately experience housing inequality, redlining and obstacles to mortgage loans, which are often insurmountable. Those he seeks to benefit with his decision are White people who see the arrival of Black residents or people of colour in their neighbourhood as negatively impacting the market value of their homes and who think these changes will raise crime levels. This is White identity politics and racial stereotyping the Black identity to exclude and deny African Americans an equal value of life choices and liberty.

Boris Johnson staked his ascendancy to, and acquisition of, the UK premiership on Brexit, running on the fumes of far-right White supremacy rhetoric and feeding the fear and grievance of the White identity politics in Britain. This includes both the politically literate and illiterate. He literally ran on the slogan 'Take Back Control', which was heavily focused on immigration. Immigration was not just about control from the EU but also about the deportation of Afro-Caribbean British people whose citizenship was unlawfully denied, such as with the Windrush generation. The Windrush scandal was a strategic 'hostile environment' executed by the UK Home Office to remove Black British nationals of Caribbean ancestry who were then detained and deported en masse from the UK, as if they were criminals and unlawful immigrants.

In February 2020, Boris Johnson insisted on deporting fifty men of Jamaican heritage who had lived in Britain for most, if not all, of their lives on the basis that they were foreign nationals who had committed crimes. In the House of Commons, he dou-bled-down on his position by telling MPs that 'the people of this country will think it is right to send back foreign national offend-ers'.* When he said 'people of this country', he did not appear to be thinking of Black British people but of White British people whose White identity politics secured him the keys to 10 Downing Street and who wanted Brexit. He gave no regard to the totality of the circumstances of each individual case but instead tore families apart and forcibly removed them from the UK. Many of them had not completed the immigration process of naturalisation and some were in the position they were in because of administra-tive errors by their parents. Despite the condemnation of the Government's treatment of the Windrush generation, they went

---

* Rob Merrick, 'Boris Johnson insists first deportation of Caribbean nationals since Windrush scandal must go ahead', *Independent*, 5 February 2020, https://www. independent.co.uk/news/uk/politics/boris-johnson-deport-caribbean-flight-win-drush-scandal-immigration-a9319336.html.

ahead to deport the Jamaican 50, clearly learning nothing from the Windrush scandal. Even the courts had held that some of those scheduled to be on the flight had been denied appropriate access to legal advice and representation. Bear in mind that non-British citizens convicted and sentenced for more than twelve months are subject to automatic deportation. However, the demographic of the population more likely to be disproportionately impacted by this are Black British people.

The Jamaican 50 deportation was racially motivated and centred on the White identity politics that demanded Brexit. This is why Boris Johnson uses words such as 'foreign national offenders' and 'serious criminals' to trigger the dehumanised Black identity as violent, dangerous and law breakers. What Boris Johnson said about the Jamaican 50 was untrue, as most were not guilty of serious crimes. The mischaracterisation only served to trigger more racial stereotyping. The Opposition leader at the time, Jeremy Corbyn, challenged Boris Johnson on his hypocrisy, asking the question at the House of Commons, 'Is it one rule for young black boys from the Caribbean and another for white boys from the US?'* Boris Johnson is known to have dabbled in class-A drugs, conspired to beat up a reporter with a friend, and was born in the United States. Would the same standard have applied to him? No.

Another legacy of Boris Johnson is ramping up the stop-and-search powers of the UK police, knowing fully well these have been and will be used disproportionately against Black British people. Being Black is the cause for Black people, particularly men, to

---

* Andrew Woodcock and May Bulman, '"One rule for black boys and another for white boys": Corbyn condemns Johnson hypocrisy over Jamaican deportation flights', *Independent*, 12 February 2020, https://www.independent.co.uk/news/uk/politics/boris-johnson-jeremy-corbyn-pmqs-jamaica-deportation-home-office-black-white-a9331201.html.

be stopped by the police without actual probable cause. During the initial Covid-19 lockdown, London police carried out 22,000 stop-and-searches on Black men between March and May 2020. 80% of these led to no further action. The application of both the UK immigration and stop-and-search policies to Black people are racist and discriminatory and are used in order to scapegoat them. *This is why I resist.*

WHITE IDENTITY POLITICS IS DIVIDE AND RULE

'Divide and rule, weaken and conquer, love and enslave, these are three tenets of politics'*

Rwandan writer and blogger,
Bangambiki Habyarimana

Boris Johnson and Donald Trump constantly employ White identity politics to drive their public appeal. They utilise the 'divide and rule' tactic reminiscent of the segregation strategy of British colonialists to cause division and stamp out consolidation of power against them. Conflict is what they thrive on to gain and maintain power in order to break up the concentrated force of non-White identities from marginalised groups. The tactic of divide and rule in politics is both tangible through direct rule and intangible by imposing division through others, particularly through Black people or Ethnic Minorities who benefit from proximity to White supremacy, otherwise known as racial gatekeepers. Writer Oliver Markus Malloy explains:

---

* Bangambiki Habyarimana, *The Great Pearl of Wisdom*, 2015.

'The rich ruling class has used tribalism, a primitive caveman instinct, to their advantage since the beginning of time. They use it to divide and conquer us. They drive wedges between us peasants and make us fight each other, so we won't rise up against our rulers and fight them. You can observe the same old trick everywhere in America today: Red states and blue states are fighting. Christians and Muslims are fighting. Men and women are fighting. Baby Boomers and Millennials are fighting. Black people and white people are fighting. That doesn't just happen all by itself. There are always voices instigating these fights.'*

Malloy's summation speaks to my earlier assertion about the White politically illiterate being on a leash led by the White politically literate to push a divisive agenda. The consequences of which will be borne by the White politically illiterate but mostly by marginalised non-White identities, particularly Black people. Look at the intersection of Red vs Blue, Christians vs Muslims, Men vs Women, etc. and Black people are disproportionately impacted. This divisionary tactic of White identity politics is used to absolve White society of institutional racism. Here are a couple of recent examples, centring Whiteness despite the global protests of Black Lives Matter. In July 2020, Arkansas Republican senator Tom Cotton called the slavery of millions of African people 'the necessary evil upon which the union was built'† in order to pass legislation to reject the 1619 Project which 'aims to reframe the country's history by placing the

---

* Oliver Markus Malloy, *How to Defeat the Trump Cult: Want to Save Democracy? Share This Book,* Becker and Malloy LLC, 2017.
† Frank E. Lockwood, 'Bill by Sen. Tom Cotton targets curriculum on slavery', *Arkansas Democrat Gazette,* 26 July 2020, https://www.arkansasonline.com/news/2020/jul/26/bill-by-cotton-targets-curriculum-on-slavery/?ne.

consequences of slavery and the contributions of black Americans at the very center of our national narrative.'* In Britain, Schools Minister, Conservative MP Nick Gibb rejected including in the curriculum shared history of Black and minority ethnic people who shaped the UK, and learning of historical injustices that led to racism today. Both politicians employed White identity politics to reject injustices suffered as a result of White Supremacy, and the assimilation of history that includes Black, Asian and Ethnic Minorities, contributions.

WHITE IDENTITY POLITICS IS RACISM

White supremacy is White identity politics and White supremacy is racism. Hence, White identity politics fuels, enables and *is* racism. White people who subscribe to White identity politics suffer from an inferiority complex of false White supremacy. Racial diversity scares them and triggers their most primal fears of inferiority. In the words of writer, Ashley Jardina, 'when you're accustomed to privilege, equality feels like oppression.'† It is no wonder that, in 2020, both the United Kingdom and America have at their helm the most overtly racist Prime Minister and President in recent history. Both having been placed there by White identity politics.

---

* 'The 1619 Project', 14 August 2019, https://www.nytimes.com/interactive/2019/08/14/magazine/1619-america-slavery.html.
† Ashley Jardina, *White Identity Politics*, Cambridge University Press, 2019.

EXHIBIT A: BORIS JOHNSON

'This is a man who is deeply prejudiced and obviously I'm horrified about the possibility that he may remain prime minister. He is fundamentally sexist and racist.' *

Michael Mansfield, QC

In the face of overwhelming protests in support of Black Lives Matter, Prime Minister Boris Johnson denied that the United Kingdom was institutionally racist while claiming the country had made significant progress on racism, both of which are false. This coming from a man who has been overtly racist in both his personal and professional life. Referring to African people as having 'watermelon smiles', he wrote as a columnist, 'It is said that the Queen has come to love the Common-wealth, partly because it supplies her with regular cheering crowds of flag-waving piccaninnies'.[†] As editor of the *Spectator*, he condoned and signed off on articles that inferred Black people had low IQs, and described African American basketball players as having 'arms hanging below their knees and tongues sticking out'.[‡] In an article he wrote in 2002, Boris Johnson stated that colonialism in Africa should never have

---

* Jon Stone, 'Boris Johnson said that seeing "bunch of black kids" makes alarms go off in his head, in old column', Independent, 22 November 2019, https://www.independent.co.uk/news/uk/politics/boris-johnson-bunch-black-kids-racist-column-guardian-a9213356.html.

† Boris Johnson, 'If Blair's so good at running the Congo, let him stay there', *Telegraph*, 10 January 2002, https://www.telegraph.co.uk/politics/0/blairs-good-running-congo-let-stay/.

‡ 'Boris says sorry over "blacks have lower IQ" article in the Spectator', *Evening Standard*, 2 April 2008, https://www.standard.co.uk/news/mayor/boris-says-sorry-over-blacks-have-lower-iqs-article-in-the-spectator-6630340.html.

ended while putting Britain forward as a White saviour to the African continent. He further asserted that 'the continent may be a blot, but it is not a blot upon our conscience. The problem is not that we were once in charge, but that we are not in charge any more.'* This is the man Britain trusts to have changed his views or who can be relied on to direct the UK on eradicating racism? How can this be the case when he epitomises everything that is institutionally racist about the United Kingdom? Boris Johnson is Prime Minister for the very reason that his views and actions encapsulate the purpose of White identity politics and White Supremacy. The evidence doesn't end there. Boris Johnson dog-whistled the first African American President, Barack Obama, by feeding the trope that Obama is more Kenyan than American when he wrote 'the part-Kenyan president [has an] ancestral dislike of the British empire – of which Churchill had been such a fervent defender.'† The claim of Obama having an ancestral dislike of the British Empire was to 'otherise' him as not American. Plus his reference to 'ancestral dislike' speaks to Kenya as a former colony of the British Empire and intimates dislike to stoke division. Additionally, Boris Johnson argued for a continuation of colonial presence in Africa by writing 'the best fate for Africa would be if the old colonial powers, or their citizens, scrambled once again in her direction; on the understanding that this time they will not be asked to feel guilty.'‡ This is the man who also wrote

---

* Boris Johnson, 'Africa is a mess, but we can't blame colonialism', *The Spectator*, 2 February 2002.

† Jon Stone, 'Boris Johnson suggests "Part-Kenyan" Obama may have "ancestral dislike" of UK', *Independent*, 22 April 2016, https://www.independent.co.uk/news/uk/politics/boris-johnson-suggests-part-kenyan-obama-may-have-ancestral-dislike-britain-a6995826.html.

‡ Boris Johnson, 'Africa is a mess, but we can't blame colonialism', *The Spectator*, 2 February 2002.

that Black kids made him turn a hair and he would put on a 'pathetic turn of speed' when he saw Black youths in the park.* In what reality would he ever recognise the injustice and inequality experienced by Black people when he denies them and surrounds himself with White people and racial-gatekeeping Ethnic Minorities who feed his rhetoric? Boris Johnson does not care for or about Black people; if anything he enforces the dehumanisation of the Black identity.

During the UK Black Lives Matter protests, he refused to take the knee, referred to protesters as thugs and waged a culture war to trigger the far-right sentiments of White identity politics, leading to visible altercations between protesters. He never once condemned Donald Trump for his racist and inflammatory comments about protesters in the US. He appointed as head of his new Race Inequality Commission Tony Sewell, the Black British man who wrote in a 2010 article that 'much of the supposed evidence of institutional racism is flimsy'.† Both his appointment and the commission set up were roundly condemned by the Black community as wrong, unnecessary and kicking the issue of racism into the long grass.

He hired eugenicist Andrew Sabisky, who believed there were 'very real racial differences in intelligence' as his No. 10 advisor. This hiring showed a strong lack of judgement and inevitably fostered concerns that the Prime Minister was, at the very least, sympathetic to these sort of views . Johnson also refused to condemn Conservative MP Craig Whittaker for blaming Black, Asian and Ethnic Minorities and Muslims for the spike in Coronavirus leading to the Government

---

* Jon Stone, 'Boris Johnson said that seeing "bunch of black kids" makes alarms go off in his head, in old column', *Independent*, 22 November 2019, https://www.independent.co.uk/news/uk/politics/boris-johnson-bunch-black-kids-racist-column-guardian-a9213356.html.

† Tony Sewell, 'Master Class in Victimhood', *Prospect*, 22 September 2010, https://www.prospectmagazine.co.uk/magazine/black-boys-victimhood-school.

re-introducing lockdown restrictions, knowing full well these comments incite racism and Islamophobia. He refused to recognise that his failure to fire advisor Dominic Cummings (after his trip to Durham for actions that stretched the lockdown rules beyond what many people thought was a reasonable interpretation of them) led to nation-wide rejection of Government advice or that it was predominantly White people who rejected facemasks, flocked to beaches and flouted social distancing rules. Instead of bringing the country together on Black Lives Matter, Boris Johnson did what he does best – divide.

EXHIBIT B: DONALD TRUMP

'Donald Trump was successful not merely because he appealed to whites' worst racial prejudices, but also because he promised to protect the status of whites. His success is a sign that in the years to come, efforts to achieve racial equality in the United States may now need to be fought on two fronts; one that addresses whites' racial biases, and another that assuages their perception of status threat and its consequences.'*

Ashley Jardina, author and Assistant Professor
of Political Science at Duke University

Trump has a long track record of being overtly racist both personally and professionally, but becoming President of the Unites States of America took his overt racism to a new level of power and abuse. He became the face of White Supremacy and anchor of White identity politics. In 2016, he described himself to the *Washington Post* as the 'least racist person you've ever encountered'. This is false. Donald

---

* Ashley Jardina, *White Identity Politics*, Cambridge University Press, 2019.

Trump is the most overtly racist sitting President of the United States. He learned to weaponise his racism, bigotry and prejudice in order to win the highest office in the land by riding the tidal wave of White Identity politics. He became the advocate of 'birtherism', the conspiracy against US President Barack Obama that claimed he was not born in the United States and hence had no right to be President. This was all in an attempt to unseat and delegitimise the first African American President of the United States of America. This attack of birtherism was White identity politics personified and launched Trump's political campaign. His entire 2016 election campaign was racist, sexist, misogynist, Islamophobic, plagued by sexual abuse allegations and run on such divisive rhetoric, but that paled in significance to that which his presidency would unleash.

The 2017 Charlottesville Unite the Right rally protest against the proposed removal of the statue of Confederate General E. Lee led to a violent altercation between protesters and counter-protesters. This ultimately resulted in the murder of one of the counter-protesters, Heather Heyer, and injured more than thirty-five people. The rally was organised by and intended for White supremacists. Protesters were openly wearing swastikas, giving Nazi salutes and protesting the cultural genocide of White people. Trump shockingly blamed both sides for the 'egregious display of hatred, bigotry, and violence on many sides.' He went on to say there were 'very fine people on both sides.' He was calling violent right-wing militia Nazi protesters 'good people' but said the counter-protesters were 'very, very violent'. In 2018, Trump called Haiti and African nations 'shithole' countries. His comment was triggered by the challenge to his decision to revoke Temporary Protected Status to hundreds of thousands of foreign nationals from countries that have suffered war, natural disaster or other humanitarian emergencies. The 'shithole' comment evidenced the racial motivation and bigotry to exclude these foreign nationals on the basis of their race. He was targeting non-White and non-European immigrants. He even asked for more immigrants from Norway, complaining that immigrants from Nigeria would never 'go back to their huts'.

> **Donald J. Trump** ✔ @realDonaldTrump May 29 2020
>
> *This Tweet violated the Twitter Rules about glorifying violence. However, Twitter has determined that it may be in the public's interest for the Tweet to remain accessible.* <u>Learn More</u>.
> . . .. These THUGS are dishonoring the memory of George Floyd, and I won't let that happen. Just spoke to Governor Tim Walz and told him that the Military is with him all the way. Any difficulty and we will assume control but, when the looting starts, the shooting starts. Thank you!

Trump's incompetent mismanagement of the Coronavirus pandemic, which left America leading the world with over 8 million cases and over 200,000 Covid-19 deaths (and counting at the time of writing) will be one of the lasting legacies of Trump's inept Presidency and administration. African Americans and Ethnic Minorities bore the brunt of the discriminatory impact of the virus, with more deaths and sickness reported from these communities. But equally unforgettable and unforgivable will be the racist, totalitarian and bigoted legacy of his reaction to the US #BlackLivesMatter protests following George Floyd's killing by White American police officer Derek Chauvin. Trump revealed himself to be a morally bankrupt fascist exploiting and politicising the fear and anger of Americans over institutional and systemic racism for political ends. Each time he opened his mouth he aggravated the situation. He even used the Holy Bible as a political prop. With every single one of the fifty united states in flames of protest, Donald Trump's tyranny further descended to silence Americans with rubber bullets and turned America into a war zone. One of the multitudes of egregious and inflammatory responses he tweeted was 'when the looting starts, the shooting starts' in May 2020. These words are loaded with the history of the American Civil Rights movement, where African Americans were injured and killed. He literally licensed the indiscriminate shooting of African Americans, knowing full well they would be injured or killed by police and military shooting. His hypocrisy was staggering given his tweet to Iran in January 2020 not to shoot its Iranian protesters.

Trump used authoritarian tactics to push a law and order agenda for his re-election campaign and occupied cities unlawfully so as to claim he was 'tough on crime'. Cities such as Portland and Chicago had federal agents dressed in camouflage military wear, armed with tactical gear, who fired tear gas, rubber bullets and flash-bang explosives into groups of American citizens protesting institutional and systemic racism against Black people. These Federal agents pulled protesters into unmarked vans in violation of their Fourth Amendment rights against unreasonable seizures. America, the land of hope and the free, was turned into a war zone again and again. He employed divide and rule tactics, stoking and triggering White identity politics to escalate the situation. Instead of de-escalating a situation and providing much-needed leadership, Trump did the opposite – he antagonised the situation and spurred on the hate and violence. A real leader, who cared about #BlackLivesMatter, would have given the American people what they want – measures to end police brutality and to instil justice, fairness and equality.

Trump suggested he was honouring George Floyd's memory by being tough in sending out the National Guard to deal with protests. But this was disingenuous, given it was police brutality that killed George Floyd. Trump supporters used the deaths of police officers David Dorn, David Underwood and the injury of Max Brewer to justify his actions. There was no justification for the deaths and injury of police officers and equally no justification for racists and Trump supporters to politicise it to discredit and de-legitimise the #BlackLivesMatter protests. There was equally no justification for unprovoked police brutality on unarmed peaceful protesters, which was a direct result of Trump's mandate to the Police and National Guard. In June 2020, former US President Obama gave much-needed leadership, reminding all talking against the protests that America was founded on protest:

'And for those who have been talking about protests, just remember, this country was founded on protest. It is called the American revolution. And every step of progress in this country, every expansion of freedom, every expression of our deepest ideals, has been won through efforts that made the status quo uncomfortable. And we should all be thankful for folks who are willing in a peaceful, disciplined way to be out there making a difference.'*

Martin Luther King Jr said it best: 'riot is the language of the unheard'.† People riot against injustice, and the injustice of racism against Black people has long been fought and resisted in America and Britain. This is why White supremacists seek to silence, discredit and de-legitimise the #BlackLivesMatter movement, because it is a protest against the institutional racism they impose. Racists

---

* https://edition.cnn.com/us/live-news/george-floyd-protests-06-03-20/h_4bee6cbe5bf2c5fcd65d303dd162a210.
† Martin Luther King Jnr speech, 'The Other America', delivered at Grosse Pointe High School, 14 March 1968.

will use any opportunity to kill, maim and dehumanise Black people. Trump enabled racially motivated attacks on Black people, weaponising the hurt, frustration and anger of Black people at the death of George Floyd to incite racism against them.

FREEDOM OF SPEECH

When the protests turned against statues, monuments and historical immortalising of Britain and America's history of slavery, both Boris Johnson and Donald Trump denounced the protests. Monuments linked to the Confederacy were targeted in the US by the nationwide protests, but President Trump defended Confederate symbols as part of American heritage, referring to them, including the Confederate flag, as freedom of speech. He signed an executive order to punish anyone who damaged these statues so that they would be punished to the fullest extent of the law. In Britain, statues and monuments were targeted too. Winston Churchill's statue was vandalised with the words 'was a racist', the Cenotaph was also targeted, while in Bristol the statue of slaver Edward Colston was pulled down. Boris Johnson condemned these acts and defended the statues, stating that attacking statues is lying about our history and protests had been hijacked by extremists.

Freedom of speech is the defence White identity politics claim to legitimise its attacks on the freedom and liberty of Black people. No monument to war veterans or statues immortalising the legacy of British and American slavery of Black people is more important than a single Black life. The Union flag or the Confederate flag is not more important than a single Black life. No desecration of monuments is as violent as the desecration of Black lives. The destruction of Edward Colston's statue represented breaking the

symbolic shackles of racism that Colston embodied. The hypocrisy of calling this act lawless and reckless is palpable when the
destruction of Saddam Hussein's statue by Iraqis was hailed as 'acts
of resistance' by Britain and America. The destruction of Colston's
statue was an act of resistance against an institutionally racist
country. It is reprehensible to justify the existence of these statues,
flags and monuments as of 'historical benefit' when the racism and
White supremacy they represent is the lived experience of Black
British people today. But this forms part of the White identity
objective to de-legitimise the benefit of racial diversity by derailing
the Black Lives Matter cause. If White people regret the shameful
atrocities of the British Empire and America in the transatlantic
slave trade of Africans and its subsequent legalisation of slavery
through the colonisation of African nations, then they must find it
abhorrent that statues of those who profited from the dehumanisation of Black people are memorialised. But there are some White
people who do not have any such regrets, who embody the White
supremacy for which millions of African lives were enslaved, raped,
killed and African nations exploited, and who will continue to do
so under the guise of 'free speech'.

Freedom of speech comes with responsibility and consequences. Our right to free speech does not give us the right to
weaponise our speech to oppress others. A person's right to express
racist, homophobic, antisemitic, misogynist, transphobic views in
the name of freedom of speech does not trump another's right to
live in a safe society where they can have a good quality of life and
choice.

In May 2020, when Twitter first placed fact-checking links
below two of Donald Trump's tweets about mail-ballots, it was the
first time the social media company had taken steps to publicly
censure the lies and misinformation spread by President Trump

about mail-ballots because it undermined the democratic process. The President's conduct in spreading such misinformation was reprehensible. He claimed mail-in ballots were 'fraudulent', said 'mail boxes will be robbed', and repeatedly stoked the flames of racism, just as he did for the 2016 US elections, when he claimed undocumented immigrants would vote en masse. It was clear that Donald Trump was undermining the electoral process by relentlessly attacking the use of mail-in ballots. His reaction to Twitter's fact-checking links on his tweets was swift and unconstitutional. He signed an executive order to remove some of the protections given to social media platforms. He said Twitter had unchecked power to edit user's views, and claimed it was 'interfering in the 2020 presidential election' and 'stifling free speech'. However, freedom of speech is not devoid of responsibility for truth and Donald Trump had lied.

CONCLUDING THOUGHTS . . .

Like many citizens, I am angry and often feel impotence and helplessness about the rising nationalism, authoritarian populism, far-right racism and bigotry, as well as far-left ideology, in Britain and America, all of which threaten the very existence of our quality of life and choice. We must snap out of our complacency, wilful ignorance, the systemic impotent helplessness imposed on us and end the laziness of media consumption. We must have the courage of our convictions and fight for the changes we want. There is no defending the dysfunctionality of the current economic, political and social system. We are in a crisis and it is time for real solutions. These solutions can only come through active citizenship. We must do away with the past, and refuse to recycle the same arguments, politics and politicians. It is not reforming existing systems steeped in patriarchy and inequality that is needed but building new foundations that break away from the structural systems that have choked us.

The systems, laws, policies and processes built to establish fairness, access to justice and economic growth now suffocate the very people they are meant to protect. Visible racism is emanating from and enabled by political parties. A system running on the far-right fumes of racism, xenophobia and bigotry only economically benefits the 1% while inciting hatred and bigotry among the remaining 99%. We have a rigged justice system that benefits the wealthy and influential but is disproportionately applied against Ethnic Minorities. In speaking truth to power, we must recognise where the power is. It is widely acknowledged that power is government and institutions, whether public or private, but more vastly ignored is that the originator of this power is *us*. We are the ones who go into government positions, lead institutions, become decision makers in corporations and influencers and so we are, inevitably, the power we seek to change. If the ideology, beliefs and choices we live by are rooted in ignorance, bigotry, racism or hatred of any form, then that is what we take into the position we lead. Power becomes corrupted and policy decisions impacting people's quality of life and choice are influenced by that individual bigotry. Can we deal with this, you ask? Yes, we can, through social mobilisation, political participation and active citizenship. Here is how:

We must mobilise! As a term, social mobilisation can mean different things to different people, but at its very core, social mobilisation is the collective engagement and action at a local and national level that influences the mass population to help improve the quality of life and choice for the many rather than the few. This could be in the form of women's marches, #MeToo, #TimesUp and/or Climate Change demonstrations to Brexit protests. In recent years, we have seen a global scale of social mobilisation that fights inequalities through one voice of the people, regardless of socio-economic background, class and race. In fact, it is the common struggle faced by the multiple inequalities experienced by marginalised groups that draws us together.

We must be political! Political participation is how citizen power affects politics. It can take different forms, such as voting in elections, petitioning, public consultations, boycotting, demonstrations, collaborating with others for a cause, helping a political campaign or donating to one, blogging about a political issue, joining an activist group and so on. Active political participation is key and critical to any democracy. Without a doubt, political participation is necessary to achieve social justice. Active political participation requires social mobilisation for impactful change that cuts across local, national and international boundaries. Social mobilisation is the force of multiple voices from multiple representations that intersect.

We must be active! It is time to be visible. It is time to stop talking and start doing. Find your position of activism and move to the front of the march (literally and figuratively). We must be the representation we want to see. We can do this by exploring how demonstrations make a difference to us and maximising different ways of intervention, from the student union to speaking up in your book group or staging an intervention in the boardroom. The importance of collective unity in action starts with our individual affirmation of the same. Too often demonstrations are claimed by White identity politics to be pointless. This is not true. It is time to build trust and break-down barriers by holding power to account, starting with ourselves. Remaining silent about injustices is not an option. We have to speak out. We are often afraid to articulate discrimination or suppression, afraid of being branded as a disrupter, and afraid of facing the truth of our complicity in voting in leaders who thrive on division. We must act on our right to identify injustice and discrimination but also align these to solutions to address them. We are pushing at a closed door and must force it to open for change.

Debate and disagreement are at the core of any true democracy but when both are fuelled by the racism, hate, intolerance and bigotry of White identity politics, and increasing neglect of the 99% over the 1%, then our democracy is a failure. It is time to stop being co-conspirators in politics of division, religion of hate, and end the complicity of our silence and wilful ignorance. We must take responsibility for electing and supporting leaders who project division and hate. Power starts and stops with *us*. Let us consciously make the decision to revolt against the tyranny of White identity politics.

This is why I resist.

8

WHEN WILL WHITE PEOPLE PROGRESS?

'What is it you wanted me to reconcile myself to? I was born here, almost 60 years ago. I'm not going to live another 60 years. You always told me "It takes time." It's taken my father's time, my mother's time, my uncle's time, my brothers' and my sisters' time. How much time do you want for your progress?'*

Playwright, author and civil rights activist,
James Baldwin

The most powerful and poignant question to close on the issue of racism perpetuated by White people is not 'When will Black people overcome?' but 'When will White people progress?' The collision course of resistance is set. Black people are forging forward, breaking down walls of silence, refusing to internalise the dehumanisation of their Black identity and overcoming centuries of barriers by any means necessary. We are moving forward by faith not by sight towards a victory of equality we will not be denied. Justice long delayed, which is justice long denied, is no longer a rhythm we will step to.

---

* From the documentary, *James Baldwin: The Price of the Ticket*, 1989.

In the words of the professor and activist Angela Davis, 'I am no longer accepting the things I cannot change. I am changing the things I cannot accept.'* So if White people don't step to the rhythm of change, they will be left behind and be in direct collision with the surge of evolving resistance. Surely you want to be one of those who history will remember and credit for creating a new legacy? A legacy where Black people have the freedom to exercise the right to be our authentic selves, to be judged by the content of our character not the colour of our skin, and to achieve equal outcomes with our White counterparts. To finish the race started by our forebears and complete the course of the giants who paved the way. It has taken generations of Black people to progress towards a freedom forcibly stolen from us centuries ago and protest against its legacy, which still reverberates against the Black identity today. The DNA of the Black consciousness has coursing through its veins generations of our ancestors, both in and out of Africa, who waited. We are done waiting. *It is time for White people to progress.*

How much time do you need for your progress? James Baldwin asked in the late twentieth century a question which still resonates powerfully in the twenty-first century. It suggests White people lack the willingness to change the status quo of White supremacy or to break the mould of oppression that feeds their prosperity. The lack of progress from one White generation to the next leaves me with no other choice but to call the slow progress of White people deliberate. Be it in the workplace, at schools, on the street or in the echelons of power, their White privilege gives them a visible advantage over Black people that they do not want to lose. Every White person, old and young, schooled or not, able or disabled, rich or

---

* Berkeley, University of California, '400 Years of Resistance to Slavery and Resistance', https://400years.berkeley.edu/videos.

poor, would never choose to be Black knowing the stigma imposed on the Black identity. *It is time for White people to progress.*

This informs my thinking that every White person understands, both consciously and subconsciously, that at the very least what it means to be Black is perceived as less than being White. Any White person who believes in equality must understand that the status quo that currently benefits White British and Americans can no longer come at the expense of denying an equal life and liberty to Black people. If White people mean to be part of progress then they must stop being part of the barrier we face but be part of the disruption that breaks down those barriers. We must remember the White allies who, from generation to generation, have also sacrificed their liberty and in some cases their lives for the causes of the abolition of slavery and the Civil Rights movement in Britain and America. But they were lone voices, just enough to make an incremental difference but not enough to dismantle the power structure of systemic and institutionalised racism. Those White people who could did so because they decided that their way of life could no longer be predicated on the denial of an equal value of life and liberty to Black people.

It has been over three decades since the death of James Baldwin, yet in truth the same issue of racial intricacies, nuances and distinctions still exist. Today, many of these appear to demonstrate what seems like progress but are, in actual fact, not progressive. Equality and discrimination laws would be deemed progress, but are, in reality, not effective in light of continuous racism, racial discrimination and the racial prejudice Black people experience economically, socially, politically and culturally today. I fear that, if he were alive today, James Baldwin would still be asking his question to White people and finding the same lackluster and often wilful denial of the need for there to be change. In fact, I suspect some White people would retort back with 'haven't we given you enough?'

James Baldwin also said 'not everything that is faced can be changed, but nothing can be changed until it is faced',* and this is the crossroads where White people stand. Any progress for a White person to dismantle racism is predicated on facing what must be changed. To White siblings, I say that means starting with you. You must face your racism, racial prejudices and bias, and scrutinise the basis for why you do what you do and why you say what you say. When you start thinking 'but that's not me', take a step back and start instead with 'that may be me'. Denial of racism feeds the status quo of White supremacy, while refusal to understand the complicit nature of White privilege blinds you to how you contribute to and/or reproduce racism whether consciously or subconsciously. Then face the institutions that speak for you, infrastuctures that enable racism for you and a toxic culture that incites otherness, division and inequality based on the colour of another's skin.

Reading this book is not the cure; it is a step towards a better understanding of race, race inclusion and racism, but more importantly understanding your role in it. As a White person, taking deliberate and conscious actions every day against racism is the cure, particularly recognising your privilege and weaponising it to dismantle White supremacy. As a Black or Ethnic Minority taking deliberate and conscious actions every day against racism is the resistance, never making excuses for it or enabling it because you prosper in some way for your self-preservation while others of your race are oppressed by it. *This is why I resist.*

'We Shall Overcome', a folk and gospel song, which then became the Civil Rights anthem, is not a cry for validation or legitimacy from White people. We require nothing of the sort. The validation

---

* Charmaine Li, 'Confronting History: James Baldwin', *Kinfolk*, 27 March 2017, https://www.kinfolk.com/confronting-history-james-baldwin/.

and legitimacy is ours and the power to establish it comes from us. 'We Shall Overcome' is a defiant pronouncement of hope against all hope that, inch by inch, step by step, and from generation to generation, change is here to stay, because we are worth fighting for. Our futures are worth fighting for. Our children are worth fighting for. Our dreams are worth fighting for. Our hopes are worth fighting for. Our Black skin is worth fighting for. We have more to gain than to lose, while White people can also gain in a world that is just, equal and fair. If you are not ready to pay the price of giving up a status quo that benefits you unequally because of the colour of your skin, you don't want to progress. *To progress or not to progress?: that is the question for White people to answer.*

ARE YOU MALADJUSTED?

'I would like to say to you today in a very honest manner, that there are some things in our society and some things in our world [about] which I am proud to be maladjusted and I call upon all men of good-will to be maladjusted to these things until the good societies realize. I must honestly say to you that I never intend to adjust myself to racial segregation and discrimination. I never intend to adjust myself to religious bigotry. I never intend to adjust myself to economic conditions that will take necessities from the many to give luxuries to the few.'*

Martin Luther King Jr

* Martin Luther King Jr, Western Michigan University, 18 December 1963, https://m.youtube.com/watch?v=zXEIYpnlxbw.

'Maladjusted' is a powerful word used by Martin Luther King Jr which, in my opinion, should be the stress test White people must pass to determine how hungry they are to progress for change. Maladjusted means an inability or failure to cope or adjust successfully with the demands of one's social environment. Any White person genuinely wanting to progress to dismantle racism and drive a force of change across the length and breadth of society must be ready to be maladjusted to the status quo that gives them the privileges of being White. If you fit the maladjusted mindset, then say boldly and unapologetically, 'I am proud to be maladjusted', just like Martin Luther King Jr did. So let me frame the question in bitesize life-scenarios, for context.

Are you maladjusted to economic inequality? Racism is not a symptom of economic inequality, it is the cause of economic inequality to Black people. There is significant economic inequality between White and Black people that has persisted and survived for generations both in Britain and America. This economic inequality is the bedrock of the capitalism that resulted from the transatlantic slavery and colonialism, wealth built on the backs of Black slaves continued in the guise of economic and financial disempowerment of Black people and the stagnation of Black businesses. Systemic racism created visible and invisible barriers that stifled their chances at upward financial mobility, decreased the chances of economic and income security, and it could also sometimes take a whole generation for a seisimic change in fortune to occur in incremental changes. Economic fallouts from recessions and the coronavirus pandemic were borne more by Black British and African Americans, in comparison to their White counterparts, because of systemic barriers faced by Black people. It means that, in comparison to their White counterparts, during times of recession and pandemic, Black people are among the first to lose their means of living and the last to get back into the workforce in times of recovery. Economic inequality exacerbated exposure of Black workers to coronavirus.

This racial wealth gap is not because Black people do not 'pull themselves up by the bootstraps' but because of centuries' worth of imposed barriers. Examples of these include redlining, discrimination in the workforce market, segregation in social privileges, schools and housing in Britain and America, and very limited opportunity for Black generational wealth to grow and accumulate. It is a stark reality of inequality. Household income of White Americans is seventeen times higher than that of Black Americans, according to the US Federal Reserve Distributional Financial Accounts.[*] When Black Pound Day[†] was launched in June 2020, in order to support the growth of Black British businesses from systemic racism, dissenting White voices rejected this peaceful initiative to level the playing field between UK White and Black Business economy.

These dissenting voices are so adjusted to the status quo of economic inequality borne by Black people for the benefit of White people that they even begrudge one day a month to support Black British-owned businesses. Never in history and to date have Black British and African Americans, as a people, accumulated or achieved wealth parity with White people. This is because of historic and contemporary systemic economic barriers. The racial wealth gap is getting wider not smaller. If this is unacceptable, inconceivable as an ongoing reality to you, and you will consciously support Black businesses, *be proud to be maladjusted.*

---

[*] Federal Reserve Distributional Financial accounts, https://www.federalreserve.gov/ releases/z1/dataviz/dfa/distribute/table/#quarter:122;series:Networth; demographic:race;population:all;units:levels.

[†] Black Pound Day, https://blackpoundday.uk/what-is-black-pound-day/.

Are you maladjusted to anti-Black bigotry? To be anti-Black is to manifest and spread opposition and hostility to Black people through racial prejudice, bias and bigotry. This can take the form of acts, language, behaviour and complicity through what is seemingly not racially motivated but actually is. For example, White people buying into racism as a commodity is anti-Black.

The sale of Agatha Christie's book, formerly titled *Ten Little Niggers*, on Amazon is a prime example. The renowned author had used this title when the book was first published in the UK in 1939. The title came from a racist minstrel song, which formed the major plot of the book. The title was too offensive to be published in the US, so it was changed to *And Then There Were None*. Amazon had the original title on sale as a rare and collectible item. Nothing of the content of this book was changed, so surely any true collector should be after the content, which is the book under the new title. But by going after the book with the title *Ten Little Niggers*, it means what is 'rare and collectible' is the racist title and not, in fact, the book's content. What is termed as 'rare and collectible' in this instance is actually commoditised racism feeding the racist appetites of some White people in the guise of collecting memorabilia. There is clearly a demand for it, which is why there is a supply of it. The sale of racist and offensive titles by Amazon demonstrated a lack of racial sensitivity by a global organisation that claimed to be progressive. Placing market value to profit over the oppression of the Black identity enables racism and spreads anti-Black bigotry. The fact that such racist-titled books made its list in the UK begs the question of the veracity of its due dilligence when conducting quality control of book titles permitted on its platform. Lack of racial sensitivity to the offence these book titles cause is anti-Black.

I called out Amazon for this sale on its platform in a tweet on 20

May 2020. Amazon eventually took down the titles but the number of these titles for sale on its platform shows that its systems are not robust enough to ensure this does not happen again. Within months of calling out Amazon for racist book titles, as well as earphones referred to as 'Nigger', imagine my surprise when MP David Lammy, who tried to buy a pair of brown shoes on Amazon, tweeted on the 3 August 2020 about being given a colour option for the shoes as 'Nigger Brown'.*

Another example of anti-Black bigotry and racism is the dehumanisation of the appearance, behaviour and intelligence of Black people as lazy, deviant, immoral, stupid, criminal and deserving to be mocked. This all feeds into the negative stereotype of the Black identity and is still rampant today in the way it is normalised in everyday language online, offline, in the media and on television. Black people today still face anti-Black and racist depictions and imagery as piccaninnies, exotic, savages, hypersexual species and buffoons because these negative perceptions underpin our experiences with White infrastructure, a White-controlled criminal justice system, government institutions, and White-owned businesses. Anti-Black imagery is still offensive, regardless of how many decades ago it was first created. It does not lose its sting because it continues to feed anti-Black bigotry and racism.

In 2020, brands like Quaker Oats decided to retire its 130-year-old 'Aunt Jemima' brand because of its racist history and racial depiction of Black people. Following the global protests triggered by George Floyd's killing, the Pepsi-owned company explained that 'as we work to make progress toward racial equality through several initiatives, we also must take a hard look at our portfolio of brands and ensure

---

* Vincent Wood, 'Amazon removes shoe description following complaint from MP David Lammy', *Independent*, 4 August 2020, https://independent.co.uk/news/uk/home-news/amazon-racism-david-lammyshoe-complaint-brogue-a9652416.html.

they reflect our values and meet our consumers' expectations".* Aunt Jemima is the 'mammy' stereotype of the happy Black enslaved women, based on a real Black woman, Nancy Green, who was dehumanised into a 'mammy' in order to sell this product to Quaker Oats consumers. Nancy Green was born into slavery. Prior to hiring Nancy Green, Quaker Oats had used imagery of a Black woman dressed as a minstrel character and wearing a 'mammy' kerchief.

Another example where we see racism surface is when we see White people demanding an equal opportunity to call Black people the N-word, because 'nigger' is used in Black music and amongst some in the Black communities. The argument being that if they can't say it because it is a hateful slur, then Black people can't use it in any capacity. This is racist and bigoted. 'Nigger' is a hateful racist slur created and used by White people against Black people. There is no circumstance in which the word 'nigger' is acceptable out of the mouth of a White person. The only exception I can think of is to denounce it, but that can be effectively done by saying 'N-word'. However, a Black person saying 'nigger' is not a slur or racist. It is anti-Black bigotry to suggest that it is. While I personally don't use the word 'nigger' as part of my vocabulary, I recognise that it has been reclaimed by some in the Black communities, particularly African Americans, to be given new meaning as they determine it to be. The use of the word 'reclaim' here is nuanced. It does not mean ownership or empowering for Black people, it just means some Black people choose to change the narrative of the word, just like the word 'queer' was reclaimed by the LGBTQI community. In my view, the N-word is dehumanising and derogatory to Black people, but its use

---

* Jordan Valinsky, 'The Aunt Jemima brand, acknowledging its racist past, will be retired', CNN Business, 17 June 2020, https://edition.cnn.com/2020/06/17/business/aunt-jemima-logo-change/index.html.

by any Black person does not justify its use by White people. Another example of nuance is that I could say the word 'nigger' to talk about personal experiences of it, its meaning, history, dehumanisation and the like. That is not me as a Black person reclaiming it as empowering or ownership. Nevertheless, in whatever context Black people use the N-word, no White person is ever justified to use 'nigger'. That's what the 'N-word' is for. It is racist for a White person to say 'nigger'.

The outrage against BBC News in July 2020 for the use of the word 'nigger' by a White reporter in reporting the racist attack on a young Black British man, left the Black British community exasperated and angry, including its Black staff. BBC rubbed salt in the wound by defending the report. It took over 18,000 public complaints, and the resignation of BBC Radio 1xtra presenter DJ Sideman, for the BBC to backtrack on its initial defence of the report, admitting it made a mistake and offering an apology in August 2020. DJ Sideman was clear that he was quitting the BBC because its defence of the report and treatment of reactions from the Black community 'felt like a slap in the face'. Use of the 'nigger' word by a White reporter would have the inevitable consequence of potentially normalising White people saying it. That is unacceptable.

Anti-Black is the root of oppression and racism in Britain and America against Black British and African Americans. We fight against anti-Black sentiment and racism every day in all of its forms of racial bigotry, racial bias and racial prejudice. In doing so we visibly and vocally call out the specific acts, behaviour, language and other insidious manifestations that shape the dehumanisation of the Black identity. If, as a White person, being anti-Black is unacceptable and inconceivable to you as an ongoing reality, *be proud to be maladjusted.*

Are you maladjusted to racial injustice? Racial injustice experienced by Black people exists in different forms in both Britain and America. A White person is either cognisant of its insidious permutations or wilfully oblivious to it. There is no such thing as being forgiveably ignorant of racial injustice unless, as a White person, you were literally born yesterday. Racial injustice exists in education, healthcare, employment and policing. The need to eradicate systemic racial injustice that exploits Black workers and families was amplified during the global protests following George Floyd's death. In July 2020, thousands of essential workers, including fast-food workers, carers and janitors, led #StrikeForBlackLives in America to put pressure on corporations to tackle systemic racism by ending the racial injustice of low pay, zero healthcare, unpaid sick leave and resisting granting employees the right to unionise.* The aim of #StrikeForBlackLives was to connect the intersecting inequalities of racial injustice and economic inequality. The protest was targeted at corporations like Amazon, Uber and McDonalds, to name a few. Workers across the country walked off their jobs to protest in solidarity, to say economic injustice is racial injustice because Black Lives Matter. Black workers are disproportionately represented in experiencing this racial injustice.

Another example of racial injustice was the deadly fire in 2017 at Grenfell Tower in the borough of Kensington & Chelsea, one of the wealthiest boroughs in London, England. Some of its poorer residents lived at Grenfell Tower and the tragedy of the fire epitomised racial inequality and racial injustice in Britain, all of which led to the deaths of seventy-two of its residents and destroyed two hundred and one households. Most of the Grenfell residents were Black, Asian or other Ethnic Minorities. The lives of these residents were put at risk for profit, their safety ignored by the use of unsafe and

---

* Oliver Effron, 'Thousands of workers to walk off the job in Strike For Black Lives', CNN Business, 20 July 2020, https://edition.cnn.com/2020/07/20/business/strike-for-black-lives/index.html.

combustible cladding on the tower. Grenfell Tower was in a racially diverse neighbourhood and the tragedy of the fire demonstrates that all lives are not treated equally. Safe housing is a human right but this was denied to Grenfell residents and no justice has been delivered to date. There is no denying that glaring structural intersecting inequalities connect the Grenfell fire in London, the killing of George Floyd in Minneapolis and the discriminatory impact of the coronavirus pandemic on Black people in both Britain and America. These tragedies amplify the long-standing systemic racism that fosters inequalities against Black people as a marginalised community that exacerbates exposure to all three tragedies.

Racial injustice is also seen in the use of immigration policies to treat Black people in both Britain and America unequally. In Britain, the 'hostile environment' destroyed many lives of the Windrush generation, who were denied their British citizenship and wrongfully deported, losing their livelihood, access to healthcare and homes, taking them away from their families to a country many had never been to or did not consider home. The Windrush inquiry into the scandal found the UK Home Office to be institutionally racist. In America, immigrants of African descent are racially profiled and detained at a comparable rate to the mass incarceration of African Americans in US prisons. There are strong interconnecting nuances between immigration policies and systemic racism. If, as a White person, racial injustice is unacceptable and inconceivable to you as an ongoing reality, do something about it. Be like Martin Luther King Jr and *be proud to be maladjusted.*

DISMANTLE WHITE SUPREMACY

'I think that it is the obligation of the people that have created and perpetuated and benefit from a system of oppression to be the ones that dismantle it . . . so that's on us.'[*]

Joaquin Phoenix

What does it mean to dismantle White supremacy? I envisage holding a god-like hammer in my hands that literally, unequivocally and symbolically shatters the steel-layered notion of White superiority. But this would not eradicate the problem of racism because that is only one half of the problem. White supremacy is the justification for the atrocities done in the name of race superiority, but institutional racism, which is the entrenched product of White supremacy, is the root that must be eviscerated. This root is what gives power to the structural constructs of power that feed inequality and injustice.

This is the system of oppression to which Joaquin Phoenix referred when he made his profound statement about whose obligation it is to dismantle the system of oppression in play today. This takes me back to the two fundamental truths I introduced in Chapter One, which are my starting point on any engagement on racism with a White person. These are:

- First, it is not the job of Black people and Ethnic Minorities to educate White people on racism perpetuated by White people. White people must educate themselves on racism they perpetuate.

---

[*] Speech at British Academy Film and Television Arts Awards, February 2020, https://globalnews.ca/news/6498842/joaquin-phoenix-baftas-speech-racism/.

- Secondly, not all White people are racists, some are, but all White people have and enjoy White privilege. This White privilege enables and enforces White supremacy.

Accordingly, White people are responsible for dismantling the systemic oppression of racism they created. 'It's on us', said Joaquin Phoenix. I agree 100%. Black people cannot be responsible for educating White people on the racism they created and benefit from. The reason for this responsibility has been discussed in detail in this chapter and preceding chapters. Whether or not you are racist or actively anti-racist as a White person, it is your responsibility to dismantle the existence of White supremacy and the manifestation of institutional racism. It is your obligation to ensure your education on racism is influenced and shaped by those who experience it. White people will never experience racism. This is not about holding White people responsible for the actions of their ancestors, but holding them responsible for the continuing legacy of those actions. The only reason institutional racism and White supremacy still exist in the twenty-first century is because White people benefit from them and the institutions they create and control reproduce it. Slavery is not a thing of the past when the stigma and fruits of it live on in the systemic oppression of Black people today. Slave masters are not a thing of the past when power and control today is White and places barriers to stop an equal share of power and control. White people must be ready to create a new legacy for progress to be birthed. However, for progress to birth they have to be part of the struggle and the struggle means being free of a legacy that creates an unfair, unjust and unequal world for the benefit of a few. The struggle will be hard, because of those White people who will refuse to let go of the reins of power and control, and those whose sense of importance is entwined with White supremacy. But like the African American abolitionist Frederick Douglass said, 'If there is no struggle, there is no progress.'*

RACISM IS *YOUR* PROBLEM

Listen up, White people! Racism and White supremacy are your problem too. In the words of Barack Obama, 'a change is brought about because ordinary people do extraordinary things.'† There is no White saviourship going on here. The concept of a White saviour is not an unknown phenomenon, and is the self-serving act of appearing to 'save' Black people. It is delusional and objectionable. I would say unequivocally to White people, it is 'your' problem to end the racism and White supremacy created by White people. You, as a White person, are not entering into a struggle to end racism for me, a Black person. Any White person who thinks otherwise would be sorely mistaken. If you as a White person cannot see or understand how problematic racial inequality and racial injustice is for you and White people, then you have a case to answer. If you are not prepared to do what it takes to build a momentum of resistance and employ your White privilege to dismantle a system created to deny others equality, justice and fairness, then you have a case to answer. If you do not understand that this entrenched structural oppressive and racist system that feeds a false notion of White supremacy is not sustainable, then you have a case to answer. If you fail to learn from the mistakes of the slavery and colonial past to the high price being paid today by Black people, then you have a case to answer. White

---

* Frederick Douglass, 1857, https://www.blackpast.org/african-american-history/1857-frederick-douglass-if-there-no-struggle-there-no-progress/.
† Barack Obama, 15 January 2009, https://youtu.be/sCAytLvtex0.

moderates often appear to think racism is not as bad as it used to be, so progressing incrementally is okay. They often portray themselves as progressive, deluded that had they lived at that time, they would have been on the frontline of abolishing slavery or the Civil Rights movement in the Jim Crow era of segregation in America or in the era of colonial Britain where signs stating 'NO Blacks' were commonplace. I don't believe this alternative universe they have concocted. We are in the midst of the Black Lives Movement and any White person who is not ready to bend the knee, literally or figuratively, to fight racism, would have done nothing in the Civil Rights movements or to abolish slavery.

Nothing regarding racism has changed. It has not slowed down, disappeared or been eradicated. The white hats of the KKK have been swapped for police helmets. Police brutality of Black people in America and Britain is just as savage, if not more so, as the lynchings and beating of Black people by the KKK and British far-right groups of the past. Segregation has been swapped for mass incarceration and immigration detention centres of Black people. Economic barriers to wealth and prosperity today are like the denial of land and property to Black people after the abolition of slavery. There is a cost to every struggle to gain the freedom that is the objective of the struggle. Black people have been paying that cost with their lives and liberties for too long. Any White person who is not ready to pay the same price we have done does not want progress. Not for themselves or for us. As I wrote earlier, Black people are not waiting for White people to progress nor do we seek validation or legitimacy from White people in order to press on to possess a freedom unencumbered by a false Black identity contrived to feed the inferiority complex of White supremacy.

If the demand for our freedom requires it to be non-violently enforced in society, then so be it, but possess our freedom we shall, by any means necessary. That means literally breaking the shackles off our feet and rejecting the burden of stigma we have borne for too long. American civil rights activist Medgar Evers once said 'freedom has never been free'* and Black people can attest to this. We are still fighting for the freedom to exercise the right to be our authentic selves, to be judged by the content of our character not the colour of our skin, and to achieve equal outcomes with White counterparts. The struggle of Black people epitomises 'freedom has never been free'.

WHITE INGRATITUDE

'Whites, it must frankly be said, are not putting in a similar mass effort to reeducate themselves out of their racial ignorance. It is an aspect of their sense of superiority that the white people of America believe they have so little to learn.'†

Martin Luther King Jr

White people's progress is impeded by ingratitude. The ingratitude that refuses to appreciate the fact that, in spite of the pain, oppression and suffering stacked against Black people, we keep trying to appeal to your humanity. Why are you not grateful Black people are not seeking vengeance or revenge for racial atrocities? We are human, just as you are, not less human. The White race appears

---

* Medgar Evers, 'Not Forgotten', *New York Times*, https://www.nytimes.com/interactive/projects/cp/obituaries/archives/medgar-evers-civil-rights.

† Martin Luther King Jr, *Where Do We Go from Here: Chaos or Community?*, Beacon Press, 1967.

to be able to carry out racial injustice with impunity against Black people without real justice being delivered to right wrongs. Even when a modicum of light is thrown our way, it takes generations. There is no gratitude that we do not do worse than protest in the name of our righteous indignation, anger and long-suffering. The lie that Africans needed White people to justify slavery, colonialism and Christianity has been told for too long. We never needed you. You needed us. If that was not the case, why kidnap and steal Black people as slaves? If White people were so self-sufficient, why not till your lands and work your plantations yourselves instead of forcing Black people to do it? The irrational fear of Black intelligence and strength was the justification for forcing illiteracy on Black slaves, and then, after the abolition of slavery, it was segregating them from White schools, and, to date, it is the unequal distribution of spending on educational institutions where Black people are over-represented. Voter suppression as well as divide and rule tactics underpin the political manipulation of Black votes. The claim that Black migrants come to take away jobs of White people is false. Institutional racism ensures this irrational fear is played out through immigration policies, which force highly qualified Black migrants to do menial jobs. The labour workforce in both Britain and America are overly represented by Black and Ethnic Minorities because White people need them in certain jobs considered low and menial. First it was denial of liberty and, when that failed, barriers to stifle economic and political emancipation became the order of the day, and still exist in various guises today.

White people mistake our courage for weakness, our humanity for inferiority, our tears for silent acquiescence, our non-violence for subservience, and our anger as pointless. You are sadly mistaken. Even when we seek justice from the criminal justice system from White violence, we are constantly denied and expressions of anger policed. Do you think Emmett Till's family would not have wanted to do unto his killers exactly what they did to him? Do you think every police officer that has committed brutality leading to the loss of life and liberty of a Black person would have continued to do so if Black people took justice into their own hands? Deliberately impeding Black British and African Americans at every turn of liberty, life and justice for centuries is surely cause for an insurrection. Yet Black people have not done anything of the sort. Time after time we seek unity, try to speak to your humanity, but time after time we are faced with mediums of democracy being manipulated by White people to impede progress, deny life, liberty and justice to Black people.

STOP BLAMING BLACK PEOPLE

Another hindrance to White people's progress is their inability to take responsibility for the systemic, catastrophic and persisting structural inequalities faced by Black people in two of the richest and most advanced nations in the world, Britain and America. It is their refusal to accept that racial discrimination imposed on Black people, as well as social barriers created to feed the inferiority complex of White supremacy, that are the cause for these intersecting structural inequalities. When all else fails, blaming the culture of Black people becomes the lie told as the reason for the inequalities instead of placing the institutional responsibility squarely on the shoulders of those who benefit from and reproduce a system that operates to promote racial injustice and inequality. We see this culture blame game used by White people on the issue of poverty and the coronavirus pandemic, where Black people are disproportionately impacted. Lawrence Mead, a professor at New York University, blames cultural differences between White and Black people for the persistence of poverty in Black communities in America. He goes as far as to accuse Black people of culturally lacking the individualistic drive to achieve personal goals, having no moral discernment about social order and being too weak to advance through education and employment. His words, published in 2020 and not half a century ago, state:

'The United States has an individualist culture, derived from Europe, where most people seek to achieve personal goals. Racial minorities, however, all come from non-Western cultures where most people seek to adjust to outside conditions rather than seeking change. Another difference is that Westerners are moralistic about social order, demanding that behavior respect universal principles, while in the non-West norms are less rigid and depend mostly on the expectations of others. These differences best explain why minorities – especially blacks and Hispanics – typically respond only weakly to chances to get ahead through education and work, and also why crime and other social problems run high in low-income areas. The black middle class has converted to an individualist style and thus advanced, but most blacks have not.'*

This fabricated, reductive and narrow-minded view is White supremacy personified. It is untrue and an obvious trope of Black people not pulling themselves up by the boot straps. It is beyond the pale that, in the twenty-first century, Lawrence Mead thinks

* L. M. Mead, 'Poverty and Culture', Soc, 2020, https://doi.org/10.1007/s12115-020-00496-1. NB This article has been withdrawn by the publisher.

that White people have a more ambitious way of life than Black people or that the presence of poverty is due to an inability to adopt an 'individualistic' trait because our cultural norms depend mostly on the expectations of others. The best counter-argument to Lawrence Mead's mischaracterisation of Black people is Martin Luther King Jr's succinct explanation of the economic empowerment between White immigrants and African Americans:

'White America must see that no other ethnic group has been a slave on American soil. That is one thing that other immigrant groups haven't had to face. The other thing is that the colour became a stigma. American society made the negroes' colour a stigma. America freed the slaves in 1863 through the Emancipation Proclamation of Abraham Lincoln but gave the slaves no land or nothing in reality . . . to get started on. At the same time, America was giving away millions of acres of land in the west and the Midwest. Which meant there was a willingness to give the white peasants from Europe an economic base. And yet it refused to give its black peasants from Africa who came involuntarily, in chains, and had worked free for 244 years any kind of economic base. And so emancipation for the negro was really freedom to hunger. It was freedom to the winds and rains of heaven. It was freedom without food to eat or land to cultivate and therefore it was freedom and famine at the same time. And when white Americans tell the negro to lift himself by his own bootstraps, they don't look over the legacy of slavery and segregation.

'Now I believe we ought to do all we can and seek to lift ourselves by our own bootstraps. But it is a cruel jest to say to the bootless man that he ought to lift himself by his own bootstraps. And many negroes, by the thousands and millions, have been left bootless as a result of all of these years of oppression and as a result of a society that deliberately made his colour a stigma and something worthless and degrading.'*

This profound analysis by Martin Luther King Jr was given eleven months before his assassination. His exacting and truthful summation of the deliberate economic deprivation of Black people is as relevant today as it was in May 1967, when he was interviewed. Hundreds of years of free labour rewarded with nothing. Black people did not just start from scratch, they started with absolutely nothing, with no fair and equitable system in place to even give them the boots by which they could pull themselves up by the straps. They were stigmatised for being Black and economically disadvantaged while White immigrants profited from a capitalist economy built on the backs and blood of generations of Black slave labour. Black people had no means to provide for themselves and were deprived for centuries of an education necessary to give them a fighting chance to provide for themselves. This did not just happen in America but in Britain too. As proven in this chapter and preceding chapters, the way in which institutionalised social barriers and systemic racism work shows Lawrence Mead's words to be ignorant, self-serving and utterly without substance. It is time to stop blaming Black people for racism created by and for White people. This insanity must stop.

---

* Andrew K. Franklin, 'King in 1967: My dream has "turned into a nightmare"', NBC News, 27 August 2013, https://www.nbcnews.com/nightly-news/king-1967-my-dream-has-turned-nightmare-flna8C11013179.

DEALING WITH EVERYDAY
WHITE SUPREMACY

First of all, White as the default of anything is White supremacy. Secondly, the way to dismantle White supremacy is to start with every day things, because White supremacy dehumanises Black people every day in overt and covert ways. It is the way things are normalised to erase Black people's presence without thought or consequence of its impact on us. Everyday White supremacy is not inclusive because White supremacy is the antithesis to diversity and representation. If White people want to progress in dismantling White supremacy, it starts with combatting everyday racism. This is aptly captured by Angela Davis:

'I would say also that for white people, for white workers, the most important thing they have to do now is combat racism. So that racism, and the fight against racism becomes the key to a broad revolution embracing all people in this country, all working people.'*

It is important to understand that everyday White supremacy can only be deciphered, understood and interpreted from the perspective of those victimised by it not by those who benefit from and reproduce it. As previously stated, White people have never and will never experience racism. Do not confuse this with prejudice or bias which they do experience.

---

* Belle Hutton, '"We have to talk about liberating minds": Angela Davis' quotes on freedom', *AnOther*, 19 June 2020, https://www.anothermag.com/design-living/12607/angela-davis-quotes-on-freedom-juneteenth-black-lives-matter-movement.

Products

Everyday White supremacy is evident in the lack of inclusivity in products we come across that cater for Whites as the primary market. This tells Black people they do not matter, but it is so ingrained that Black people do not even expect to see products that match our aesthetic needs. Take a look at skintone-matching plasters, which have predominantly been sold as pink or beige. This is all I knew growing up and, like many other Black people, it never once occurred to me that these can be in any other colour but pink or beige. This is how White supremacy manifests itself. The design of the product clearly caters for White skin not Black or Brown skin. It is sold to us to get our money, but they cannot be bothered to provide a selection of options that cater for all skin types. White supremacy excludes non-White people and this is clearly evident in the pharmaceutical industry, when even the design of contraceptive tone patches cater to the aesthetic and discreet needs of White women and not Black women.

There is a sense of belonging and satisfaction from getting products that are not only fit for purpose but look like they belong on our skin. There are small businesses who sell skin-toned bandages and undoubtedly they would have faced structural barriers that would impede start-up, growth and/or competition against White default positioning of products. These non-White products tend to be sold at a premium, and having to pay more for something that matches and suits our Black skin is White supremacy. It undercuts the market and businesses of those businesses trying to cater for non-White markets. However, one of these small businesses is owned by a White American father who was inspired to start a company selling skin-toned plasters because he could not find plasters that matched his African American son's skin. This is an example of a White person trying to dismantle White supremacy. Think about 'flesh'-coloured products. Did you have to use flesh crayons or wear flesh tights? These products cater for the White flesh colour and not Black skin. That is prioritising the White skin over non-White skin by placing preferential value on it.

There are so many other everyday examples, from how products are advertised to who is used to model the products, from what type of product to where such products are accessible and available. I remember when my last born, then four or five years old, asked me why the kids she saw on the TV adverts for toys were White. She asked 'aren't the toys for me too?' It literally broke my heart. It was not until then that it occurred to me that at such a young age my child would pick up on this covert racism. This is White supremacy.

Language

White supremacy polices the English language and accents used to speak the English language. For instance, as a Black British woman of African descent, I have found that my 'Britishness' is often questioned because I speak English with what is viewed as a non- English accent. I was born in London and lived here for over twenty years, but my right of belonging is questioned because I don't sound 'English'.

Within the United Kingdom, various dialects and accents of the English language exist depending on where you live or come from, so there is no such thing as an 'English' accent. Even the Queen of England does not speak the English language with the same accent as most of the general public, but while there is classism and discrimination against the way some White people from regional areas of Britain speak, it is not racism and nothing compared to the stigma Black people experience.

No one's language, dialect or accent is better or worse than another's. Yet even in this, Black people are discriminated against.

White supremacy imposes a standard accent on how the English language should be spoken. Anyone speaking English with an accent that falls short of this is discredited and discriminated against. Black people have also been told 'they don't sound Black' or are met with surprise that they can speak the 'Queen's English'. The latter is perceived as the English language spoken correctly by educated people in Britain. Not only do Black people experience racism with the policing of our accent in speaking English, we also experience classism and other intersecting discrimination over this.

In America, the African American Vernacular English (AAVE), also known as Black English, is used to discredit and discriminate against African Americans. It is not perceived as speaking 'good' or 'proper' general American English and stigmatises them as not fitting in or as not smart. White Americans speaking in a different dialect or southern drawl do not face the same stigma or discrimination. Not all African Americans speak just AAVE, but they speak both AAVE and general American English. It is similar to West Africans: we speak both British English and Pidgin English, which is derived from the English language and spoken in West African countries such as Nigeria and Ghana. British English is the official language of anglophone countries colonised by Britain, such as Nigeria. The AAVE is not bad English as perceived by White Americans, but they continually discredit it by referring to it as 'ghetto talk' or 'ebonics', coined from ebony and phonics. These are racial slurs. AAVE has a very rich documented history and is a legitimate dialect of the American English language in its own right, borne from the history of slavery. The default of spoken English being a certain standard and in a set accent used to discriminate against Black people is another example of how institutionalised racism works. This is White supremacy.

Education

Education is knowledge and knowledge equals power. For the longest time, White supremacy has wielded power over what is taught, how it is taught and whose side of the story is told. This has gone a long way to fostering institutional racism, racial prejudice and racial bias. When history and culture are centred on Whiteness, this is White supremacy. This is why decolonising the school curriculum will help in dismantling White supremacy.

Decolonising the curriculum simply means to broaden national understanding of what is being taught in different disciplines by confronting and challenging colonial and Eurocentric teaching, which has long been normalised as the superior source of knowledge and has therefore influenced our societal practices today. In Britain, decolonising the curriculum would address the structural legacy of colonialism, which in most parts excludes the whole picture of what it cost to build the British Empire on the backs of slaves and the exploitation of the British colonies, particularly African nations. In America, decolonising the curriculum means to centre the consequences of slavery and the contributions of African Americans in its historical narrative. Attempts to decolonise education and introduce wider shared thinking that is representative of diverse contributions, which differ from the normalised White British and American contexts, are rejected as being racially divisive.

British and American children must be taught *all* of their history, without exclusion, especially the brutality, deaths, blood and sacrifices of slavery that were the human cost that built the foundations of the British Empire and America. These are not inconvenient truths. Refusing to teach Black and White children their shared and diverse history, which contributes to present-day

Britain and America, is a dereliction of duty. Leaving generations upon generations of Black people to keep having the same conversations with White people on race, racism and race inclusion is the direct result of the failure to teach White parents while they were at school. This leaves the next generation of Black children having the same conversation with White children, in a vicious cycle of deteriorating race inclusion. The exhaustion of this cycle is not only deep in our souls but the trauma is also deep in our DNA. Dismantling White supremacy will eradicate the power it wields over the education of generations, ultimately reshaping how Black history, Black contribution and Black heritage is taught and perceived. This means rejecting the non-representational and inaccessible positioning of Whiteness as the primary source of knowledge or as the arbiter of truth, both of which it is not, but instead embracing diverse thinking and shared knowledge to broaden our societal perspectives.

WHITE FATIGUE

Let's talk about the inevitable fatigue White moderates start exhibiting after they feel they have 'done their bit' for Black people or simply just had enough and don't want to talk or hear about racism any more. This epitomises White privilege. Having the choice to step out of the fight to end institutional racism at any time you want while Black people have no such choice is a privilege. Black people can't check out because White supremacy and institutional racism are our lived experience 24/7 and 365 days a year. Note that these White moderates are not fatigued enough to step away from the benefits they get from an oppressive system that denies Black people an equal value of life and liberty. This is because that is what their way of life is predicated on. White fatigue enables and reproduces White supremacy.

I would say to all White people reading this, it is not progress if you exercise your privilege to step out when Black people are very much still in it. Check your White privilege and nip the fatigue in the bud if/and/or the thought crosses your mind to 'take a break'. If you as an individual know that racism is wrong, then know that every time you rest, pause, or take your eye off the ball from being actively anti-racist, you are enabling White supremacy. Institutional racism and the systems that enable White supremacy don't impact all Black people the same way. Some Black people will experience levels of racism that others will never see and vice versa. Yet, in a call for solidarity, it is imperative for most if not all Black people (excluding racial gatekeepers) to fight the beast of inequality and injustice that seeks to dehumanise our Black identity. This is also true for White allies. Not all White allies will be impacted by the same levels of urgency and understanding that active anti-racism needs, but it is imperative for most if not all White people (excluding racists) to fight the beasts of inequality and injustice that result from the inferiority complex of a false White supremacy.

Well-meaning and good-intentioned White allies find that being an ally is much bigger and more intense than right is good and bad is wrong. It is literally a war of good versus evil. The harder work comes from navigating the grey shades of racism that have been normalised and crystallised in people's thinking, teaching and narrative that have become the intersectional fabric of our society. For these White allies, it will literally be a mind distorter, because it will destabilise their current notion of reality and upend their beliefs. There are no superheroes here, just ordinary people who lead, and that leadership can be Black and White as long as it is a force for good, regardless of socio-economic status and political affiliation.

Dear White allies, it is also important to understand that White fatigue is another barrier for Black people to combat. It becomes a gatekeeper against progress and is equally devastating, because White allies who appear to commit to progress become gatekeepers who hinder progress due to their fatigue. The complexity and intensity of institutional racism becomes too much of a responsibility, or perhaps they were never truly committed in the first place, because at the first sign of a hurdle they refuse to go further. The silence and inaction that results from White fatigue enables and enforces White supremacy. Your fatigue must not come at the cost of denying an equal life and liberty to a Black person. Be consciously intentional about not letting that happen.

WHITE PERFORMATIVE ACTIVISM (ALLYSHIP)

White performative activism is White supremacy. It centres Whiteness not just by its insincerity but also by its shallow content. Performative activism says, 'Look at me, a White person supporting a Black person, I'm an ally'. It is pretend allyship with absolutely no intention of making a difference except to profit by association from the public awareness of a critical Black issue. Performative activism is performed by both individuals and institutions. Jumping on the bandwagon because #BlackLivesMatter is trending, when you really don't care, is fake and damaging to the cause, so do not do it. Black people will not hesitate to call you out on the hypocrisy. Active anti-racism is so much more amplified today through social media and the use of mobile phone cameras that performative allyship and activism is unequivocally called out for doing damage, however unintentional it may be.

White performative activism is another form of exploiting the pain and struggle of Black people. It is hijacking a profound time of the cause or movement for self-gain with no follow-through. Once the trend has passed, these performative allies disappear and, much worse, withdraw the much-needed resources and support that their apparent presence promised. I would go as far as to call performative activism abusive. It is neither pertinent nor relevant if the outcome of abuse was intentional; when a White person or institution fakes allyship to a Black cause, the message is clear – you don't care, and we don't matter. Performative activism is not anti-racism. It furthers the cause of White supremacy by its blatant disregard of the lives and liberty of Black people at risk from their fake allyship. Acting out the motions of activism to gain social capital by association with a worthy cause pertinent to Black people is inherently bad. It is careless and shows reckless contempt for the inherently complex issues of institutional racism being addressed for Black people. So, whether that was your intention or not, White performative activism makes you part of the problem not the solution.

On race-related issues, White performative activism sows distrust in an already tenuous relationship between Black and White people regarding our lived experiences of institutional racism. The death of George Floyd and outbreak of the global #BlackLivesMatter protests highlighted the serious problem of White performative activism in real time, with the severe backlash from Black British and African American communities against the perpetrators. What we saw were some White people, celebrities, brands and corporations from different industries visibly pledging their undying support for the #BlackLivesMatter movement, especially by posting Black squares on social media. Some even going as far as bending the knee. The solidarity being expressed by some of them raised significant eyebrows considering the pregnant silence of these people, brands, and corporations before the emergence of this movement and particularly how they had treated Black people close to them previously. Undoubtedly this behaviour towards Black people close to them fed the lived experiences of institutional racism of those Black people. Just as bad were what appeared to be White allies using social media to fake acts of support in the #BlackLivesMatter movement. Going with the flow with activism without understanding why and what you are being an activist for undermines any good intention you may have. It is lazy to think that it is understandable when it is not. Think about the generations of people who have done exactly this and set back progress. Let's look at some examples.

When Black British Trans activist and model Munroe Bergdorf was dropped in 2017 by L'Oréal as its first transgender model for calling out racism, she summed up the experience with words that resonate with every anti-racism activist: 'The most ridiculous thing is that you call out racism and they respond with more racism. It just doesn't make any sense.'* Three years later, L'Oréal posted support for #BlackLivesMatter, stating 'Speaking Out is Worth It'. There was an immediate severe backlash, given the way the brand had treated Munroe Bergdorf when she called out racism and White supremacy following the death of an anti-racist protester by a White supremacist at a 2017 rally in Charlottesville, Virginia. Munroe did not hesitate to call L'Oréal out for its hypocrisy, gas-lighting and refusal to talk about racism at the time. What is clear is

---

* Nosheen Iqbal, 'Munroe Bergdorf on the L'Oréal racism row: "It puzzles me that my views are considered extreme"', *Guardian*, 4 September 2017, https://www.theguardian.com/global/2017/sep/04/munroe-bergdorf-on-the-loreal-racism-row-it-puzzles-me-that-my-views-are-considered-extreme.

that Munroe was dropped in 2017 for talking about the very issues of racism and White supremacy that led to George Floyd's death in 2020. L'Oréal didn't consider these issues righteous enough to support in 2017, but given the significant PR opportunity #Black-LivesMatter presented three years later on, it now supported these issues. L'Oréal's treatment and immediate rejection of Munroe Bergdorf when she spoke out against racism revealed a brand that was going with the flow with what side of public opinion it should take. It sowed distrust and its blatant demonstration of performative activism for #BlackLivesMatter was the last straw – the backlash was strong, loud and unequivocal. You can't support a movement when you don't support even one Black life the movement speaks for. To its credit, L'Oréal expressed regret, sought reconciliation with Munroe Bergdorf, and appointed her to sit on the company's Diversity and Inclusion board to help direct them going forward.*

When African American football quarterback Colin Kaepernick started the national anthem protests in 2016 by refusing to stand up during the national anthem but instead taking the knee to protest police brutality and injustice facing Black people in America, he explained that:

> 'I am not going to stand up to show pride in a flag for a country that oppresses black people and people of color. To me, this is bigger than football and it would be selfish on my part to look

---

* Rob Picheta, 'L'Oréal dropped this model for commenting on systemic racism. Now it wants her back', CNN Business, 10 June 2020, https://edition.cnn.com/2020/06/10/business/munroe-bergdorf-loreal-rehired-scli-gbr-intl/index.html?utm_term=link&utm_content=2020-06-10T15%3A50%3A03&utm_source=twCNN&utm_medium=social.

the other way. There are bodies in the street and people getting paid leave and getting away with murder.'*

While sportsmen and women being at the forefront of Civil Rights activism and social justice is nothing new, Colin Kaepernick raised awareness around issues of social injustice that should have been addressed in America long ago and it cost him his professional career. His actions were largely condemned by the National Football League (NFL) and President Trump, who politicised it by criticising those who knelt during the national anthem as disrespecting the flag. Colin Kaepernick was blackballed in 2017 when he was not signed up by any of the NFL teams and accused the teams of collusion to keep him off the field. NFL then banned on-field kneeling during the national anthem in 2018, instead demanding that all players stand up and show respect for the flag.[†] However, following George Floyd's death, the NFL rallied round the #BlackLivesMatter movement and pledged its support. It did a U-turn and, in June 2020, removed the ban on bending the knee during the national anthem in protest against racism. The NFL explained that they were wrong not to listen to NFL players and encouraged all to speak out and peacefully protest. As would be expected, there was a strong backlash at their hypocrisy, given Colin Kaepernick was denied his professional football career for speaking out against racism, and the public demanded that the NFL apologise to Kaepernick.

---

* 'Colin Kaepernick protests anthem over treatment of minorities', The Undefeated, 27 August 2016, https://theundefeated.com/features/colin-kaepernick-protests-anthem-over-treatment-of-minorities/.
† Kevin Breuninger, 'NFL bans on-field kneeling during the national anthem', CNBC, 23 May 2018, https://www.cnbc.com/2018/05/23/nfl-bans-on-field-kneeling-during-the-national-anthem.html.

CONCLUDING THOUGHTS . . .

Life, liberty and justice are inalienable human rights and sacrosanct. White people who want to progress on race inclusion with Black people must be consciously intentional about eradicating White supremacy and the institutional racism created to enforce it, which means being actively anti-racist. They must always remember that racism is their problem too. Progress comes with a price tag, a human cost that Black people have paid with their lives and liberty for little justice. If you, as a White person, are maladjusted to this status quo then be ready to pay a price. If you don't want to do what it takes to progress, then stay out of the way of progress, but remember that resistance to progress is futile. We will get there with or without you.

Being anti-racist is a life choice. It is active not passive, vocal not silent. It is intolerant of injustice. It is ever present always. It is a lived experience not a difference of opinion. Anti-racism has colour – the unifying colour of all races that transcends the division of racial bigotry, racial prejudice and racial bias that fuels the condemnation of difference. Anti-racism is not politicised to the left, right or centre. There is no variation or exception to what is anti-racist. Anti-racism is humanity – it fights for the humanity for all without denying humanity for some.

Life, liberty and justice underpin our democracy in Britain and America. Enshrined in the 1776 American Declaration of Independence are the words: 'We hold these truths to be self-evident, that all men are created equal, that they are endowed by their Creator with certain unalienable Rights, that among these are Life, Liberty and the pursuit of Happiness.' Enshrined in the UK Human Rights Act are: (Article 1) Right to Equality; (Article 2) Freedom from Discrimination; (Article 3) Rights to life, liberty and personal security;

and (Article 4) Freedom from slavery. The intent is clear that life, liberty and justice should belong to all. However, the application of the provisions and protections of these rights and freedom have long been subjected to a hierarchy based on race, so that Black people and people of colour in both Britain and America have had their rights to life, liberty and justice violated or withheld with impunity.

Racism determines who enjoys the rights and freedoms that should by nature belong to all. Black people are in the unenviable position of having to justify our freedom to a right and the right to the freedom to exercise those rights. The justification for an inalienable right, which we should not have to prove, is diminished by a system that does not recognise our rights because it judges and sees us through a lens that dehumanises our Black identity as less than human and unworthy. It is an uphill struggle, especially for those without the means, power or influence to do so. This should not be a struggle. It is a man-made imposed oppression on those perceived to be weaker and inferior. There is no place for this injustice and denial of life and liberty in our world today. This is the big picture that every White person must face. You have the responsibility of eradicating anti-Black racism in Britain and America, which not only has devastating consequences for Black people, but also for White people. Progress is inevitable: be part of it. Fatigue is not an option. Be consciously and intentionally anti-racist, both individually and institutionally.

CONCLUSION

IT'S TIME FOR
A CONSCIOUS REVOLUTION

'Those who make peaceful revolution impossible will make violent revolution inevitable.'*

Former President of the United States of America,
John F. Kennedy

It is time to fight back. Revolution is the absence of an evolution of humanity. There is no justification for the monopoly of power to be White or centred on Whiteness. There is no justification for a Black or non-White person who reaches the echelons of power, in any social, political or economic context, to centre Whiteness and pull up the ladder behind them. Responsibility lies with every single one of us. The time for that responsibility starts now. A revolution is inevitable, and it is up to us (Black and White) to decide if it will be peaceful or agitated. Agitated does not necessarily mean the oppressed will employ masses of firearms. No. However John F. Kennedy is correct that revolution can be violent. After all, Martin Luther King Jr led a revolution where violence was committed by the oppressors (White), not the oppressed (Black), which then

---

* Remarks on the first anniversary of the Alliance for Progress, 13 March 1962.

led to ending segregation and enshrining voting rights for African Americans. Revolution can come from a combination of sources, including technologically, digitally, or in some other sense the twenty-first century presents. What is certain is that the revolution will not be by words alone. The fact that a White person, regardless of socio-economic status, would not trade places with a Black person suggests they may be afraid of what retribution looks like if the same was done unto them as has been done to Black people for centuries.

The below observation by African American theologian James H. Cone captures the indignity of what Black people have to deal with, which also aptly demonstrates the extent to which White people have not progressed:

'The most sensitive whites merely said: "We deplore the riots but sympathize with the reason for the riots." This was tantamount to saying: "Of course we raped your women, lynched your men, and ghettoized the minds of your children and you have a right to be upset; but that is no reason for you to burn our buildings. If you people keep acting like that, we will never give you your freedom."'*

As was the case decades ago, these exact sentiments are being said today by some White people regarding the outrage, pain and demonstrations held by Black people to address the injustice of racism and discrimination experienced. Absolutely nothing has changed with some White people's attitude towards equality for Black people. This quote is reminiscent of what is being said about the #BlackLivesMatter movement and global protests against police brutality

---

* James H. Cone, *God of the Oppressed*, Seabury Press, 1975.

today. Does this sound familiar to you? It does to me. In the words of Bernice King, 'there is no form of protest against racism that is acceptable to racists'.*

The expectation that Black people must move the hearts and minds of White people to be free from institutional racism is racist and White supremacy. The expectation on Black people to centre Whiteness on how *we* respond to injustice is racist and White supremacy. The expectation on Black people to 'wait our turn' or wait longer because we are not a priority, is racist and White supremacy. The expectation that White people set the timing of our priorities is racist and White supremacy. The continued denial of our lived experiences of racism, is racist and White supremacy. Centring Whiteness as the standard for professionalism, culture, way of life, choices of lifestyle and the like is racist and White supremacy. White people setting and dictating the parameters of our protests is racist and White supremacy. White people placing conditions on the human dignity and individual freedom of Black people is racist and White supremacy.

Watching or being oblivious to the dehumanisation of the Black identity and witnessing Black people enduring violence meted out by White people and White-controlled institutions against our life, liberty and justice will no longer be tolerated. We see this violence as physical, mental and spiritual, a violence that is visible and invisible, a violence that permeates through society – socially, culturally, economically and politically. A violence that desecrates Black lives more devastatingly than pulling down flags, kneeling during the national anthem, or pulling down statues or monuments that immortalise the legacy of slavery and institutional racism. White people and institutions then having the caucasity to react to Black people's response

---

* https://twitter.com/BerniceKing/status/1304256639403544576?s=20.

to their violence by intensifying racism in all of its forms against us is racist and White supremacy.

Black lives and liberty cannot be replaced. The fact that some people say 'let the democratic process run its course' epitomises the laziness, indifference and ambivalent attitudes shown to those different from them, knowing full well this would never be their own personal experience. These people know the democratic process is weaponised to delay and deny justice for Black people, slowly but surely frustrating those it is meant to serve and protect, particularly those of working class without means or influence. So, I ask you, what democratic process? Both British and American democratic processes must be revamped from the inside out, thoroughly detoxed from centring Whiteness at its core, for it to be a democratic process that serves and protects all rights and freedoms for and of all.

If not democracy, which America and Britain pride themselves in, how about the fact that both pride themselves as Christian nations? With 'In God We Trust' on US currency and officially using expressions like 'God bless the United States of America' or 'God bless the Queen' and the Queen being the Head of the Church of England. However, surely the case could be made that they are paying lip service to Christianity with both countries' history of injustice, slavery, segregation, denial of justice, inequality as well as loss of life and liberty to Black people and Ethnic Minorities on the grounds of superiority of race? Compassion and humanity is in very short supply, especially when it threatens the way of life built on enforcing White supremacy and predicated on the denial of an equal value of life and liberty to Black people. I find this analogy from James H. Cone between the cross Christ died on and the lynching tree used to hang Black people particularly insightful:

'The cross can heal and hurt; it can be empowering and liberating but also enslaving and oppressive. There is no one way
in which the cross can be interpreted. I offer my reflections
because I believe that the cross placed alongside the lynching
tree can help us to see Jesus in America in a new light, and
thereby empower people who claim to follow him to take a
stand against White supremacy and every kind of injustice.'*

This analogy is spot on but it also reveals that religious bigotry
comes in all forms and is used to commit some of the most heinous crimes the world has seen. I am a Christian and know that
Christianity has been used to justify the superiority of the White
race, slavery and legitimise the indignities Black people experience.
This abuse of Christianity has nothing to do with the faith I know
to be true. There is no Biblical justification for institutional racism
or White supremacy especially as the Christian faith preaches that
to love your neighbour as you love yourself is the second greatest
commandment. There is no Christian love for Black people in racism
or White supremacy. To conclude, I am going to use the parable of
the sower to solidify the need for all people, regardless of race, to
be consciously intentional about eradicating White supremacy and
institutional racism. This is what we need for real progress. However,
I am also realistic about my expectations of people's intentions', as
this parable of the sower aptly describes:

'A farmer went out to sow his seed. As he was scattering the
seed, some fell along the path, and the birds came and ate it
up. Some fell on rocky places, where it did not have much soil.
It sprang up quickly, because the soil was shallow. But when

---

* James H. Cone, *The Cross and the Lynching Tree*, Orbis Books, 2011.

the sun came up, the plants were scorched, and they withered because they had no root. Other seed fell among thorns, which grew up and choked the plants. Still other seed fell on good soil, where it produced a crop – a hundred, sixty or thirty times what was sown. Whoever has ears, let them hear.'*

Which seed are you? This parable aptly demonstrates what it means to be actively anti-racist. For ease of reference, you and I are the seed, and the knowledge we have drawn from this book and others like it, is the soil. The first seeds that fall on the path are those people who hear about racism but don't understand or care about it so do absolutely nothing. The seeds that fall on rocky places with little soil are those people who are performative activists with no substance and, once Black lives are no longer trending, they fall away and do absolutely nothing. The seeds that fall among the thorns are those who want to be actively anti-racist but their way of life is predicated on the benefits of White supremacy or proximity to it, so this lures them away and they don't last. But the seeds that fall on good soil are those who are maladjusted to injustice and inequality, those who understand the urgency for change, and those who are ready to prioritise the lives and liberty of others. They immediately pursue active anti-racism and make a difference. I fell on good soil. I am anti-racist and believe in one race – the human race.

This. Is. Why. I. Resist.

---

* Matthew, 13: 1–9, New King James Version (NKJV).

ACKNOWLEDGEMENTS

As a woman of faith, let me be true – I could not have written this book without God. Each time I faced a blank sheet and wondered how I could possibly transfer the inner workings of my mind and thought process on to the page, God showed me how and brought the words to life in this book. God alone is my strength and my perfection. This book is a balm to my soul, and was both emotionally exhausting and exhilarating to write. Thank you, God.

Writing this book would not have been possible without those who have helped to shape my life experiences; those who fought the good fight for racial equality and justice; those who paved the way for voices like mine (both contemporaries and those whose shoulders we stand on); and people young and old from different backgrounds who have been a source of inspiration to me. Thank you, all.

A special thanks to my husband and daughters, who put up with my drama while writing this book for six weeks. Their sigh of relief when my first draft was submitted was palpable! LOL! A special thanks also to my parents, Prince Adebajo Babington-Ashaye and Mrs Morenike Babington-Ashaye. I hope they are proud of who I am today. To my dear editor, the lovely Katie Packer, who heard my voice and believed what I have to say must be published – thank you.

To my literary agent, the phenomenal Cathryn Summerhayes, who did not hesitate for one second to represent my voice – thank you. To all those who will be impacted by this book and go forward to positively disrupt the status quo in order to end racial injustice and inequality – thank you.

To wrap up, I want to thank me. I thank yesterday's me for fighting through my fears and doubts, for giving the me of today a book I'm proud to have written, and opening new doors for the future me because of the actions I took yesterday. I thank me for coming out on the other side to see what is possible to achieve when I believe in me.

INDEX